# Deep Purple
## STORMBRINGER

Laura Shenton

"I think *Burn* is the vibrant sound of a brand new band but *Stormbringer* was made by a band that has found its feet. By now we were writing great songs, we were in the zone."
**Glenn Hughes**

# Deep Purple
## STORMBRINGER

Laura Shenton

WYMER
PUBLISHING
Bedford, England

First published in 2021 by Wymer Publishing
Bedford, England www.wymerpublishing.co.uk Tel: 01234 326691
Wymer Publishing is a trading name of Wymer (UK) Ltd

Copyright © 2021 Laura Shenton / Wymer Publishing. This edition published 2021.

Print edition (fully illustrated): ISBN: 978-1-912782-60-4

Edited by Jerry Bloom.
Proofread by Lin White of Coinlea.

The Author hereby asserts his rights to be identified
as the author of this work in accordance with sections
77 to 78 of the Copyright, Designs & Patents Act 1988.

All rights reserved. No part of this publication may be
reproduced or transmitted in any form or by any means,
electronic or mechanical, including photocopying, or any
information storage and retrieval system, without written
permission from the publisher.

This publication is sold subject to the condition that it shall not,
by way of trade or otherwise, be lent, re-sold, hired out or
otherwise circulated without the publishers' prior consent in any
form of binding or cover other than that in which it is published
and without a similar condition including this condition
being imposed on the subsequent purchaser.

Every effort has been made to trace the copyright holders of the
photographs in this book but some were unreachable. We would
be grateful if the photographers concerned would contact us.

eBook formatting by Coinlea.
Printed and bound in Great Britain by
CMP, Dorset.

A catalogue record for this book is available from the British Library.

Typeset by Andy Bishop / 1016 Sarpsborg
Cover design by 1016 Sarpsborg.
Cover photo © Jeffrey Meyer (Pictorial Press / Alamy Stock Photo).

# Contents

*Preface*   7

Chapter 1: *Why Stormbringer?*   11

Chapter 2: *Before The Storm*   17

Chapter 3: *The Making Of Stormbringer*   41

Chapter 4: *Mk3 As A Live Band*   61

Chapter 5: *The End Of An Era*   91

Chapter 6: *Stormbringer Is A Worthwhile Album*   113

*Discography*   141

*Mk3 Tour Dates*   151

Deep Purple - Stormbringer: In-depth

# Preface

Deep Purple's *Stormbringer*! What an album! It's a fascinating album in terms of how it seems to significantly divide opinion between fans and even the band themselves. In writing this book, I think it's really important that I present this album objectively. In order to do that, I'll start by putting it out there where my bias sits with the album. I think it's fantastic! I feel that it was of its time and it is an enjoyable insight into what Deep Purple were doing at a time when they had not long proven themselves as a new line-up (Mk3). The band were at the height of their success as a supergroup and *Stormbringer* was made at a time when commercially it made sense to continue working together.

But of course, that's just my opinion and it's certainly not that which this book is framed upon. For of course, the purpose of this book is to represent what *Stormbringer* meant to Deep Purple as individuals and in terms of their legacy overall. In such regard, this isn't going to be the story of what *I* think the album sounds like, that would be boring, I'm merely the narrator here.

It is the case that many consider that *Stormbringer* had many things going against it. When I put my music historian's hat on, it seems very apparent that when *Stormbringer* was made, Deep Purple were not getting on well socially and it was probably something of a strain to work together professionally. Although time had been set aside to make the album, individual band members were not united in their vision of where they wanted to go with it. Of course, the end of Deep Purple Mk3 signified the beginning of Rainbow and *Stormbringer* is an essential ingredient in that aspect of Deep Purple's history. And thus, the purpose of this book is to examine those things in detail. I want to revisit the narrative surrounding *Stormbringer* because it is an important album in Deep Purple's discography.

As with any band, every member will have a different opinion on each of the albums they put out. As a result, I think it is tremendously important not to generalise. As someone who has no affiliation with Deep Purple or any of their associates, in writing this book, I will be doing everything I can to quote good, reliable sources that will help to get the story of the *Stormbringer* album across with as much authenticity as possible. Due to this, you'll be seeing lots of quotes from vintage articles. I think they are important to document anyway because there will probably come a time when stuff like that gets harder to source.

This book is a gossip free zone. I want to present facts rather than all kinds of weird and wonderful speculations. Also, there will be nothing herein that is in the lexicon of "this song is in B minor so it probably means XYZ." Nope! Not Happening! I want to present what Deep Purple experienced with *Stormbringer* and not what I did as one of millions of fans out there. Oh, and that reminds me, I was born in 1988 — so blummin' ages after all of this stuff happened and thus, this book is a culmination of extensive research that I intend to use objectively to offer a worthwhile narrative on what is, ultimately, a very worthwhile album.

Deep Purple - Stormbringer: In-depth

# Chapter One

## Why Stormbringer?

*Stormbringer* is such an interesting Deep Purple album because it is so eclectic. It contains such a diverse mixture of funk, soul and blues. Love it or loathe it, *Stormbringer* is an important part of Deep Purple's discography because it is reflective of a band that were at a critical point of exploration and indeed change. The hard and heavy rock sound that fans, the media and particularly Blackmore were most drawn to wouldn't really be implemented again until the regrouping of Mk2 Deep Purple in 1984 for the *Perfect Strangers* album. Mk3 Deep Purple was a very different band in many ways. With Glover and Gillan out and Hughes and Coverdale in, the musical influences that contributed to the writing and playing of *Stormbringer* were drastically different to what people may have expected from Deep Purple, particularly in view of the four Mk2 albums, *In Rock*, *Fireball*, *Machine Head* and *Who Do We Think We Are*.

As the first Mk3 album, whilst *Burn* featured a few hints at the soul and funk influences of Hughes and Coverdale, it wasn't really until *Stormbringer* that it became so tremendously evident that Deep Purple had moved so significantly far away from what their initial musical remit was with the introduction of Gillan and Glover for the first Mk2 album, *In Rock*. When a band takes a new direction musically, sometimes it is met with open arms by fans, the media and indeed, the band themselves. But there is always that element of risk. It is a risk because when a band defies expectations musically, it can be a challenge for all concerned, particularly if they are not one hundred per cent behind such change themselves. This was certainly the case for one Ritchie Blackmore who, post *Stormbringer*, decided that the funk and soul directions of the album were not something that he wanted to be part of.

It was reported in *Circus Raves* in January 1975; "Deep Purple is one of those bands that can provoke the natural elements into a frenzy. Ritchie Blackmore, his reddish mane whipping through the dramatic storms of plectrum chordation evokes ancient Druidic madness. Keyboard magnus Jon Lord, as well as vocal dead-raiser David Coverdale, bassman Glenn Hughes and earth moving skinman, Ian Paice, complete a line-up mesmerising enough to freeze oceans or heat glaciers. While this quintessential experimenters in the lab of heavy metal sound toured the American continent putting a foliage of wattage on the bare branches of the late autumn trees, their newest album was being mixed down for the last time back in Europe. The title track of *Stormbringer* is about a whirlwind creating chaos wherever it goes and it is a fitting opener for the meteorological conditions which spring up whenever Purple appears, and is heard. Yet like the temperate climate between the two zones of Cancer, *Stormbringer* is not all strum und drang. Although a definitive Purple rocker, the new LP has some mild warm moments which suggest that there is a partial soulful thaw in the sound of Purple."

It could be said that there is a poetic irony on the album art of *Stormbringer*. Released in November 1974 and Deep Purple's ninth studio album, storm clouds are gathering over the horizon. Just months earlier, the Mk3 line-up of Deep Purple had overcome the challenge and scepticism of having a hard act to follow in the form of the Mk2 line-up and yet, with *Stormbringer*, as one of the founding members of the band, Ritchie Blackmore had swiftly reached the point of disinterest

## Why Stormbringer?

in his own group and decided to call it a day and went off to form Rainbow with a new set of musicians. In particular, the funk and soul influences in *Stormbringer* were very much down to the newer members of Deep Purple, David Coverdale and Glenn Hughes. The pair's enthusiasm for such musical style had been present as far back as their formative years as musicians. It was evident in Glenn Hughes' band, Trapeze, and it was certainly evident on the *Stormbringer* tracks, 'Love Don't Mean A Thing' and 'You Can't Do It Right (With The One You Love)'. As had been the case on *Burn*, released just nine months earlier in February 1974, Coverdale was on lead vocals with Glenn Hughes contributing a significant amount of his own, sometimes doing backing vocals and occasionally doing lead, as on 'Holy Man'.

Mk2 had shared the writing credits on their albums, but with Mk3, songs were credited individually. Coverdale has writing credits on all of the songs on *Stormbringer*, with other tracks on the album credited to mixed combinations of the group (see the discography in the back of this book for detailed personnel information, track listing and tour dates).

*Stormbringer* strongly represented a change of musical direction for Deep Purple. Whilst everyone contributed well in terms of technical musicianship, it was ultimately the album that broke the Mk3 line-up of Deep Purple and cost the band the brilliance of Blackmore's guitar skills. Now whilst Blackmore is certainly not the only good guitarist to walk this earth, his influence on and contribution to Deep Purple was to the extent that for many, *Stormbringer* marked the end of an era for the band.

In November 1974, the UK album chart offered lots of musical variety, but there was certainly no shortage of interesting content for rock fans. By the 23rd of the month, Elton John's *Greatest Hits* debuted at number one and new entries in the top ten included Sparks' *Propaganda* and Queen's

*Sheer Heart Attack*. It was in the same week that Deep Purple's *Stormbringer* entered at number twelve. It reached number six in its second week in the chart and by 1975 it had been certified Silver. On the American album charts, *Stormbringer* reached number twenty. Not bad but not as successful as *Burn*. However, *Stormbringer* still fared well and with Deep Purple having a loyal and much larger audience in America by that point, it went Gold.

It could be considered that the success of *Burn* was such that *Stormbringer* had a tough act to follow. Whilst Mk3 Deep Purple was, if not by name, a new band, they didn't struggle with *Burn*. It got to number three in the UK and number nine in the USA as well as number one in several European countries (it went Gold in the UK, US, Germany, France, Argentina and Sweden). Much of the album's content was also incorporated into the stage show, including one of the group's most memorable live performances at the California Jam in April 1974. Not only was *Burn* a very successful album, but in terms of live performances, Mk3 Deep Purple, love them or hate them, good reviews or bad, still seemed to be at the top of their game in 1974. Certainly to an extent that making another album, which just so happened to be *Stormbringer*, warranted.

Although the soul and funk influences were there on *Burn*, it was on *Stormbringer* that they really came to the fore. By this time, Coverdale and Hughes had gone from being the new recruits to being respected musicians and members of the band in their own right. Glenn Hughes stated in his 2017 edition autobiography; "We weren't the new boys anymore. We had our own minds and our own thoughts." It was reported in *Sounds* in November 1974; "Now that Purple are well established into their third phase, things seem to be well on the move again. Their music has now taken a new direction and a great deal of the credit can be taken by the two new additions, Glenn Hughes and David Coverdale."

## Why Stormbringer?

It is worth noting that as much as Blackmore seemed unhappy about the musical direction that things went in with *Stormbringer*, it doesn't seem to be the case that he wasn't open to change at all. He was quoted in an interview with *New Musical Express* in 1973; "We make music for other people to listen to, and a lot of people liked Ian (Gillan) singing. It was just that after four LPs I personally — I can't speak for the others, I don't know how they feel about it — I was tired of the vocal sound of it. So the others said they agreed, and we all got together and Ian said he wanted to resign. We thought that was fair enough, because this was our chance to get a new vocalist. We've just progressed naturally. We haven't tried to set any barriers because we're not into that. I've just been living on and playing the music I want to. I wouldn't stay with the band if I wasn't satisfied with myself... I wanted to leave basically because I didn't think the vocal side of it was happening at all. It was quite nice but it was too poppy. Now, it's more into a blues-commercial pop thing. Our new singer has a more masculine voice, and with Glenn we hope to get a double type of feel. You could say a Beatles feel with a hard rock backing is the basic thing. There are now two other guys involved, so it makes it more or less a new band to me. It's not Deep Purple anymore, although it's still the same name. Really, it's a completely different band."

Of course, it is now known that the reasons behind Mk2 Deep Purple splitting (for the first time!) went a bit deeper than just musical differences. There is a good range of literature on that one already but basically, too much touring combined with the pressures of not having enough space from each other resulted in confrontations that concerned all of Mk2; the dynamics of the band were such that Gillan and Glover were the casualties of that, at least until Mk2 reformed for *Perfect Strangers* in 1984. But the point remains that by the beginning of the Mk3 line-up, Blackmore didn't seem to be against a change of musical direction, even though it was ultimately that which played a big part in him not being too pleased with *Stormbringer*.

It can be enjoyable for fans to hear something different from their favourite bands but essentially, it was the new musical direction for Deep Purple that played a large part in the personnel conflicts that would ultimately see the breakup of the Mk3 line-up. Success has never been enough to ensure line-up stability of any band and that was certainly the case with Deep Purple. This is fascinating and certainly warrants discussion. *Burn* did well. *Stormbringer* did well. Commercially and musically. And so this therefore raises a question of "what went so wrong with *Stormbringer*?" "Why was it the straw that broke the camel's back in terms of Blackmore leaving the band?" "Why does the album seem to divide opinion so much today in terms of the band's historic discography and legacy?" The purpose of this book is to look into those things in detail.

# Chapter Two

## Before The Storm

With Ian Gillan and Roger Glover out of Deep Purple, things hung in the balance as to whether the band could continue their tenure with a new line-up. Whilst Glenn Hughes and David Coverdale were recruited to the band relatively soon after Gillan and Glover's departures, there was no certainty that musically and commercially, Deep Purple would be in a safe position. According to Hughes, Deep Purple had had their eye on him for some time. He was quoted in *Record World* in June 1976; "(Deep Purple) were planning for me to join in 1973 but they asked me at the end of '72 to join. I had to think about it because I had my own group, Trapeze, and I wanted to make it on my own, with my own group. After a while I studied Purple's music and I got to know the guys really well so I became interested in what they were doing and what they were going to do. I was interested in the new format of what it was going to be at the time."

Hughes was quoted on how he came to be in Deep Purple in *Sounds* in January 1974; "It started about a year ago. Trapeze were playing in Miami Beach while Purple were on vacation. We were both staying in the same hotel and we met and we were playing some gigs in the same area and we used to go and see each other. I never knew they were checking me out, so it came as a complete surprise. I was a bit wary about it because at first I said no and yes. I said no because I wanted to sing, I didn't care about anything else except although I love playing bass as well but I wouldn't play with anybody if I couldn't sing, because I love singing. They (Purple) said it was okay because I would be singing and after that I went through a very horrible phase after the first month I had joined 'cause they were looking for a singer, but they wanted two singers, but soon things became clearer and I realised they wanted to change the Purple sound by having two singers."

Hughes was quoted in the same interview regarding his move from Trapeze to Deep Purple; "I was really happy with them, the only difference now is that now I'm getting treated better, I've got more money, which I don't give a damn about because I've got lots more years to worry about something like that. But the thing is it got to a stage with Trapeze last year where it was so good and so tight but we weren't getting anywhere at all. We did nine tours in America and we were just breaking it in some areas and that was after three years, there was no hope."

So whilst musically Hughes was in a good place with Trapeze commercially, joining Deep Purple was too good an opportunity to turn down. Hughes continued in the same feature; "When I was with the band (Trapeze) for three years I kept on saying 'I'll give it another year' and we did nine ten-week tours in America, that's enough to break any band. The thing was in the States we didn't have any agency and we couldn't back any big bands so we were doing shit gigs all the time. It got us together musically but it screwed us up physically. I used to go to hospital to get shots, we were never big enough to cancel gigs. I love that band, I shall always want to be associated with them no matter what they do I'll always want to jam with them 'cause I love them." Hughes was quoted in *Disc* in May 1974; "Trapeze worked mostly in the Southern part of the States because we couldn't have survived on what we could earn here (Britain). So this really (with Deep Purple) is my first tour of Britain."

## Before The Storm

Before he joined Deep Purple, David Coverdale was in a band called the Fabulosa Brothers. He was quoted in *Sounds* in November 1974; "That was a lovely time, a bunch of guys, they've unfortunately split up. When I left the band, they all just sat around. We were really together socially and the drag was that I had been told to keep the Purple auditions to myself. I felt such a bastard because we were always being very open to each other. I've always been with the same nucleus of musicians, I was also restricted because there were a lot of people I would have liked to have worked with but I couldn't because I couldn't afford a PA system or mic... With equipment and somebody steering us it could have been as fine as The Average White Band, it was very much that way. It was difficult then because when you're a semi-pro musician you have to play what the audiences want, but we got away with so much because we took established standards and twisted them about a bit. Some of the ideas we had were terrific but there were so many restrictions as far as employment was concerned. Members of the band had businesses and I'm not going to turn around to anybody and say stop what you're doing and go on the road because I know it can be a heartbreaking experience and a financially breaking one at that. But I'll certainly be indebted to the people I worked with because they were on the tape which made me sound better than I was — I was drunk."

At the same time Coverdale also explained how he got to join Deep Purple; "I was reading the papers and I saw that Purple were still looking for a vocalist. I didn't think about it, every week someone's looking for a musician. The chick who worked at the boutique I was at was a Purple nut... The chick there took out a copy of *Machine Head* and put it on and half a dozen guys came into the shop, one of them came up to me and said 'are you still singing?' like you'd say 'are you still brushing your teeth?' or something like that and I said 'Yeah' and he asked 'why don't you go for a job with Purple?' and laughed. I got really depressed and then I got really violent and thought 'I don't want to be regarded as a joke, it means a lot to me' and then I remembered I knew this chick who knew Purple and I tried to get in contact with them."

That didn't work out but, as Coverdale explained in the same feature, "Then I got a friend of mine, Roger Barker, who used to be manager of the Redcar Jazz Club, to take over for me, I rang him up and I said 'I'm going after the job with Purple' and there was a deadly silence. Everyone I had told had faith in me but that was like aiming my sights a little too high. I think they thought I should have started a little lower down the scale... So Roger Barker said leave it and I was just left sitting around. After a couple of weeks we got a phone call from one of the secretaries at Purple's office who asked me to send a tape and a photograph around. I thought I might as well forget it because I didn't have any photographs, and the tapes I did at Strawberry Studios sounded great on the night but they were so bad in the cold light of day that when I mixed them it was dreadful. The band sounded great but I just turned round and said 'forget it' because it was so bad. There were a lot of good parts but with me being so drunk it sounded terrible. So I sat there thinking 'dreadful' and then I had a brainwave when I was recording a copy tape. I turned the volume down on the bad bits to make it look as if there was a fault and it worked. Purple were attracted to the tone."

Just over a year after his audition with Deep Purple Coverdale recalled; "We did a couple of old rock things, which was embarrassing because I didn't know the words, I wasn't around at the time. I learnt 'Smoke On The Water' and 'Strange Kind Of Woman' and they didn't play either of those. It was supposed to be a two-hour audition but we played for hours just blowing like hell. This was the first time I met them so I was meeting people I had just been reading about — stars mate. They were great, very natural people. Glenn was ace. He was

## Before The Storm

late to the audition because he got lost in the traffic coming down and he came in, his hair all over the place. He has amazing hair and these Easy Rider Polaroids and he strolled in with this big shoulder bag and guitar case. I was getting nervous and I sat there waiting. They all wandered through for a blow and I heard this funky sound and I thought 'what's that?' it was the same kind of stuff I had been playing with the Fabuloso Brothers. I joined them and began to shout to get rid of all the butterflies, like when I go on stage now and shout 'alright?' it's to get rid of my nerves 'cause the audience scream back. Audiences are the best dope in the world. Anyway, we went through a few rock numbers and then we stopped and Jon Lord went out to listen to it because it was being recorded. He came back and said it sounded good. Then Ritchie turned to me and said 'look you can sing rock, let's see what you can do with melody' and we had a go at 'Yesterday' and it came out really nice."

When asked what his feelings were upon joining Deep Purple, David Coverdale was quoted in *Record World* in June 1976; "Acute surprise. I didn't expect to get the job to be quite honest. I listened to a couple of things before going to see them. *Deep Purple In Rock* really impressed me. I still think it's a classic album for its time, and they've sustained it now. I didn't think my tonsils would be the sort they were looking for, but I knew they had a record company and a stable of artists and I thought I may be able to impress them enough to have heard something like 'you're not the sort of vocalist we're looking for but we could use you as an artist in the studio…' We arranged an audition in Scorpio Studios in London and I went down to the studio as nervous as hell with a bottle of brandy. I've got a lot of confidence in myself, otherwise I would never have suggested an audition, I'd never even stand on stage if I didn't have confidence in myself. But it's weird, standing there with a bunch of stars — but they were great, very human, and that's one of the things possibly that made the transition from singing salesman to fronting a band a lot easier, because the guys were very human."

Apparently, the letter that David Coverdale sent to Deep Purple was the one that was transcribed in *New Musical Express* in November 1974; "Dear Sir, I heard that Ian Gillan is leaving Deep Purple and my friends persuaded me to send in a tape. Please excuse the quality but I hope you'll give it a listen. My phone number is on the tape box if by some small chance you want to speak to me. Regards, David Coverdale."

As the reporter advocated of the letter in the same feature; "Coverdale's letter of application for the situation then vacant in Deep Purple certainly doesn't exude an aura of either burning ambition or single-minded self confidence. But a struggling semi-pro singer who worked by day in a boutique probably believed it'd take more than a demo tape, letter and snapshot to bring about an exchange between the drab interior of a Redcar shop and the bright lights of superstardom in the Metropolis. So naturally, there's a reticent and embarrassed air to the letter. Whether by mercy of providence or merely in recognition of an enormous talent, Coverdale's approach was, as you know, successful. A speculative gambit paid off. And having just celebrated his first anniversary with the band he is in a position to clarify his intentions behind the letter by comparing it to another missive received recently by Purple."

Coverdale was quoted in the same feature; "There was a guy who sent a tape of "Black Night" with piano accompaniment and a letter saying 'Dear Deep Purple, I'm not very good looking but me Mam thinks I am. But I would like to sing with your group because I think it would be great. I'm going to play "Black Night" now' and the band were really touched, although obviously it was very naïve. It could have paid off. I sent mine in with the same intention. When I came for the job with Purple I didn't expect to get it, but I would have liked it. I knew they had their own label and their own stable of artistes, and I was hoping for a job as a songwriter. But obviously I would have preferred the job singing with the band, but I didn't expect that my throat was the one they were looking for. And I certainly didn't have that sort of image."

Jon Lord was quoted in *New Musical Express* in April 1974; "It was around the time of the (Mk2) Japanese dates that we knew it was all over. We already knew Roger was leaving and had asked Glenn to join us. Then these tapes started arriving from prospective singers. More than five hundred of them. We listened to the first one hundred and fifty and got more and more disillusioned. Some of them were hilarious, most of them were awful and would have made worthy Monty Python material. Some came with really strange letters like the one guy who said 'I'm very good looking, at least my mother says I am. I've had no experience but I know I could be a star and get the girls excited.' Then Dave's tape arrived and it stuck out like a diamond. He was doing 'Everybody's Talkin'' with his mates from the Fabulosa Brothers and it was a really strong masculine voice that we knew was right."

Ian Paice was quoted of the newly established Mk3 line-up in *Melody Maker* in December 1973; "We were looking for more freedom, not to expect the same thing every night. We're not knocking Ian Gillan because the way he did it was very good but a change is a rest. We've had a rest and we've changed, so it can't be bad. We knew David (Coverdale) was good. His tape was the best that came in so we got him down. We did the studio audition where he was very nervous but we took that into consideration. We just jammed... We are louder than we were before. We are now geared, equipment wise, to playing massive venues. You can't just say turn it down because it doesn't sound the same. In the contracts we sign, it says "to appear as known" — we are known as the loudest band in the world as the *Guinness Book of Records* says. We may be the loudest they have ever measured but compared to people like Grand Funk and Black Sabbath we're quiet man! Now our sound is a lot more lyrical than it was before. We still keep it punchy but it's a lot more 'songy' whereas before we'd take a theme and just blow on it, now there are more songs and a lot more vocals. It's, how can I say, a more musical act. It's definitely the complete Deep Purple — again."

Even before *Burn* was released, it was a given, at least within Deep Purple and their intentions as a band, that Mk3 were not aiming to explicitly replicate what Mk2 sounded like. Glenn Hughes was quoted of the recently established Mk3 line-up in *Sounds* in January 1974; "It felt as if I'd been playing with Ian (Paice) so many years, because he's so tight it's a great feeling. It's like a new band, they've still got the three main guys in Purple. Ian Gillan and Roger (Glover) were great but the original Purple were Ian Paice, Ritchie and Jon who I think are incredible and gave myself and David an opportunity and we took it. It's a fight because some people want to hear the old songs, we do two old songs but apart from that it's all new stuff and the majority of people reacted well. After only a few gigs I think it's great! There wasn't any bother about me because I had played a lot of American gigs but the biggest worry was David because he was taking Ian Gillan's place. We're singing together but he is taking his place on stage. Ian Gillan, as well as being great looking, had great feeling on the stage, that's what they were worried about but he's worked out all right."

Coverdale was quoted in *Rolling Stone* in November 1975; "When Glenn and I joined back in chapter three, we were told that we were not replacing Roger Glover and Ian Gillan. We were joining musicians who played under the name Deep Purple." Glenn Hughes was quoted in *Sounds* in January 1974; "They (Mk2 Deep Purple) always wanted to play with a little bit more bluesy feel and now it makes you want to shake your arse and I think that's why they changed their line-up. I think everyone's excited about this band, the album, the gigs. From the past few concerts I know people are coming to see the new Deep Purple and that's great."

Still though, the legacy that had been put in place by Mk2 was undeniable. When *Disc* introduced David Coverdale as Deep Purple's new singer in September 1973, the legacy of Mk2 was still substantial; "The band's *Machine Head* album, still high in the US chart after one year, receives a Platinum disc for sales of two million dollars. Their current album, *Made In Japan*, has already been awarded a Gold disc." It was reported in *Sounds* in December 1973; "German EMI held a reception for the band who were presented with engraved gold watches for the sales of *Made In Japan* ('It's a bit embarrassing receiving a gift for something you didn't play on,' admitted Glenn). The reception also marked the band's release of a double compilation, *Mark 1 & 2*. The material includes a beautifully arranged version of the Beatles' 'Help'."

Fortunately, that was an admin thing and certainly not the fault of Coverdale and Hughes as new recruits. Besides, although they had joined a band with an already rich legacy by then, it turned out that they were capable of bringing their own capabilities to Deep Purple. Glenn Hughes was quoted in *Disc* in May 1974; "Dave and I get on really well, even though we're both singers... Not a single person has shouted 'we want Ian' or anything like that. I wouldn't dream of putting him down but that's a great relief to David and I... I've been amazed at the incredible response we've been getting everywhere — it's quite frightening seeing those kids milling around in front of the stage, screaming."

It was reported in *Sounds* in December 1973; "No one's denying that Gillan and Glover were major forces in the old guard but they seemed to come to a standstill after *Machine Head* and it was generally known all was not quite right regarding the compatibility of the band members. Purple have developed a helluva lot more of what Ian Paice describes as "balls", the two new members are better than I'd imagined and while I'd always admired Glenn Hughes' work in Trapeze, I didn't expect the very funky feel he's injected into the band."

For context, this was reported on at the time when *Burn* had been recorded but not released and the Mk3 line-up were still becoming accustomed to playing live together. The feature continued; "Like Glenn, Dave (Coverdale) also has a love for soul music and an extremely powerful voice with a lot of depth and guts. By the time Purple reach Britain, Coverdale will be able to prove his virtuosity as a singer and performer and he's already acquired a great number of European fans. Back on stage the new numbers are so tight they have to be seen to be believed. Purple played a lot of material from their new album, a recording that will make up for a lot of disappointments on their *Who Do They Think They Are* (sic) album. Ritchie has always been acclaimed as a technical player but never as one with enough feel but that's another thing that can be dismissed. He comes over as a very tasteful blues guitarist and this is highlighted in a tasty number titled 'Mistreated' with all the emotion and feel you want. As a showman he can't be faulted either, contorting his body to those bent guitar notes, raising his arm high in the air and watching the band out of the corner of his eye to see that everything's working perfectly. More crowd eruptions when Jon Lord announced they were going to do one of Purple's old numbers — 'It was written in 1736, hope you like it', a pregnant silence and then Ritchie delicately plays a flurry of notes that lead into the instantly recognisable chords of 'Smoke On The Water'. Glenn and Dave shared the vocals — a very powerful combination — and Paice played a very energetic drum solo featuring some good phasing through the right and left hand bank of onstage speakers. The set culminated with 'Highway Star', a stunning climax featuring solos from each of the band, Glenn constantly strutting back and forth, flicking his long mane of hair back out of his eyes and playing solid, mean bass with a wah-wah attachment. Jon Lord followed with some skilful switching from mini Moog to electric piano and Blackmore put the final seal on the gig by hurling his Stratocaster into the air, catching it a split second before it hit the stage, dry ice swirled again and it was only seconds before they were into the inevitable encore."

Whilst fans and the media's expectations were such that Mk3 would never have been immune from comparisons being made with Mk2, there was an excitement in the new line-up and it is likely that it contributed to the band's productivity when making *Burn*. Glenn Hughes was quoted of recording *Burn* in *Sounds* in January 1974; "It took ten days which is great, it was exciting to do — we used to spend all night playing. It was recorded in Montreux, Switzerland, and most of the cuts were done in two or three takes. I'm knocked out with the album, it sounds great when it's loud. When we mixed it and then listened we were knocked out with it."

In *Melody Maker* in December 1973, Hughes was quoted of one of the *Burn* recording sessions; "The others went out for a meal and Dave (Coverdale) and I sat in the studio and both sang together. It was the first time I'd ever got up on anybody else singing. We both feel the same." In its infancy, it comes across that socially, the Mk3 line-up of Deep Purple happily socialised outside of work. Glenn Hughes was quoted in *Sounds* in January 1974; "We rehearsed three weeks in this castle on the Welsh borders everyday and were always together. When I'm in London I stay at Ian's."

*Melody Maker* reviewed *Burn* in February 1974; "A new epoch opens for Deep Purple with this, their tenth album. Seeming to have lost direction over the last year, even tiring, the group have returned in an avenging mood. Their two new members, David Coverdale and Glenn Hughes, have injected new fire. They're the third change of singer and bass guitarist since '68 and the sleeve notes are at pains to underline the new lease of life. It's certainly the most important album Purple have made since *In Rock*, which was a milestone in itself. Recorded at Montreux, using the Rolling Stones' mobile studio, *Burn* represents the sound and quality for which Purple seem to have been groping for more than a year. There's still that familiar malevolent potency, but it's more richly and subtly defined with greater emphasis on melodic structure. Hughes and Coverdale's elated vocal harmonies are a tour de force in their own right. They share all the songs except the seven minute 'Mistreated', the apogee of the album. The track begins at a lazy sinister pace, Coverdale tearing out the words in convincing misery, and guitarist Ritchie Blackmore excelling himself in Turkish scales. Gradually there's a movement, a shift in the bass lines and drums and suddenly, the song soars into a near-symphonic finale with chorale-like voices. The album opens with the title track, which crackles with energy, drummer Ian Paice straining at the leash, the force of the new vocal line-up immediately apparent. The erotic beauty of Blackmore's playing squeezes at the emotions, Paice kicking on the beat with tremendous vigour and racey timing. There's also the first hint of synthesiser, one of the group's new sounds. Side two erupts into 'You Fool No One', guitar bubbling like short wave static, and on the following track, 'What's Goin' On Here', Lord plays some funky piano, which is another departure for Purple. Lord generally lays back on organ, but in his piano solo things really start to swing, Blackmore playing ninths with aplomb. The final track is a surprise and something quite different for Purple — an instrumental titled simply 'A 200' featuring synthesiser and in bolero style, displaying that odd Moorish influence Purple have also had. A smothering album that's so good for the spirit and destined to be surely one of the major records of '74. The smoke's still coming out of my stereo."

*Burn* was reviewed in the Australian paper, *Hamersley News* in July 1974; "*Burn* is enough to dispel any doubt about

Deep Purple's future which may have been raised when Ian Gillan and Roger Glover left the band last year. In fact, the sound is virtually the same, although perhaps a fraction more commercial on some tracks. David Coverdale's powerful vocals make the loss of Ian Gillan nothing to worry about with classic examples being shown on both the title track and 'Might Just Take Your Life'. Ritchie Blackmore shows his usual brilliance on guitar in several solos throughout the album with a more than adequate backup from the band's new bassist, Glenn Hughes. Deep Purple break away from their conventional rock style to dabble in the blues on 'Mistreated' where Coverdale is able to show another side of his vocal prowess. As was the case with *Machine Head*, *Burn* was recorded in Montreux, Switzerland with the Rolling Stone's mobile unit. Another winner from Deep Purple! Who do they think they are?"

There seems to be a strong narrative (not just in this book, but generally) that *Burn* was a much loved album and the start of an exciting new direction for Deep Purple. It's a predominantly agreeable narrative considering how well the album did commercially but equally, the new line-up of Deep Purple and indeed, another Deep Purple album entirely, was not to every critic's taste. *Burn* was reviewed in *Rolling Stone* in April 1974; "Deep Purple's first album since last year's departure of vocalist Ian Gillan and bassist/composer Roger Glover is a passable but disappointing effort. On *Burn*, new lead singer David Coverdale sounds suitably histrionic, like Free's brilliant Paul Rodgers (rumoured to have been Purple's first replacement choice). But the new material is largely drab and ordinary, without the runaway locomotive power of the group's best work. The title track is a notable exception, attractively energetic, with appropriately speedy instrumental breaks. And 'Sail Away' is a Free-like mesmeriser. 'Mistreated' again sounds like that lamentedly extinct group, but is flaccidly lengthy (7:25). They fill out the LP with the relentlessly mediocre single 'Might Just Take Your Life', the stodgy bluesrocker 'What's Goin' On Here', the commonplace Cream-like funk riffs and harmonies of 'You Fool No One', and with a tedious Moog/bolero instrumental retread applying the coup de grace. Much of the LP is skilfully wrought and likable, and the new line-up has potential. But the Gillan/Glover spark that created 'Highway Star' and other memorable Purple smokers is regrettably absent."

Also, in June 1974, *Rolling Stone* stated of *Burn*; "Cream was schizophrenic. Like so many sixties British bands, they derived their instrumental style from American bluesmen, but they achieved their contemporary sound by recording the rock songs of bassist Jack Bruce. These were painfully humourless compositions, often devoid of intelligible melody and sung in an oppressive style that overemphasised not just an occasional word, but every word. Cream was one of the most influential of all rock bands, but Bruce may have influenced as may singers as Clapton has guitar players. Many British rock band vocalists sing (to one extent or another) in that same insensitive manner — which is why I have trouble listening to some groups whose instrumental work I admire. Deep Purple has been around a long time, but in their current incarnation they perpetuate Cream's schizophrenia. They display considerable command of their instruments (if little originality) but it's wasted behind the caterwauling of new vocalist David Coverdale, who sings some of the most godawful lyrics yet pressed onto vinyl with idiotic seriousness. On the group's behalf I note that they avoid the flip side of the worst of British rock, the wimpoid (sic) ballad. In fact, when they are burning instrumentally and everyone sings together (making the words easier to forget), they come up with a handful of acceptable, even pleasurable moments."

In contrast to the band's previous tours, 1974 was the year that Deep Purple were given the best chance possible to tour in a way that was well organised and where possible, luxurious.

Money was spent liberally to ensure that hotel bookings were completed effectively and that press attention was guaranteed. On top of that, music and sound equipment was upgraded and travel was done in limousines and where needed, a customised Boeing 707 that was affectionately given the name of Starship One. It was put together by a team in LA who ensured that it contained, within the scope and limitations of the plane, a lounge, a bedroom, a shower, a fireplace and a study. The intention was to make the plane look and feel more homely and less like a plane.

The spring tour of 1974 saw Deep Purple play Madison Square Garden as well as the famous California Jam in April. It is perhaps the case that their performance at this show became more famous as a result of Blackmore's destruction frenzy but that said, musically, it was an incredible performance too. There is a lot of literature already out there in terms of Blackmore's antics following the organisers' demands that Deep Purple went on before sundown despite what the contract said. The iconic footage was captured by ABC TV for all to see. Importantly, though, it could easily be just as iconic purely for the scale of the gig and what it meant in terms of the extent of Deep Purple's commercial success by that point in the band's tenure.

It was reported in *Circus Raves* in January 1975; "Deep Purple have been weathered by a season of hail and criticism. On strictly musical terms, it has been a rough chore for those with a grudge toward the band to slag the new Deep Purple on any musical basis, but those with a chip on their shoulder scoured up excuses to say nasty things about the band, particularly Ritchie Blackmore. Ritchie was haunted by accusations, for instance, by Emerson, Lake & Palmer regarding the Summer Jam concert. And he had a lot of things to get off his chest regarding this incident."

Blackmore was quoted in the same feature; "They said we pulled a moody when we wouldn't go on, but that isn't strictly true. We were the headliners of the show — it was written into the contract — and we were supposed to go on the stage at dusk, specifically at 7:30pm. We arrived early to the gig to tune up and sort everything out, allowing ourselves an hour, but when we got there, the promoter comes up to us and says 'you've got to go on' — we outright refused, it was 6:30 and we weren't about to do anything of the sort. He started threatening us so we slammed the door in his face. So we get accused of pulling a moody for that — that's a lot of bull. We were really pissed off about that whole gig because they had all these cameras set about and the kids who were sitting in the audience couldn't see a thing. They had paid their fifteen dollars — and that's a lot of money for someone to pay — and there were all these cameras in their way, so I started smashing things up, y'know, the usual… It's not right that they spend all that money to see us and then we have to do a bum gig, or there are cameras in the way. I used to hate American audiences, but now I've begun to really dig America. I used to get sick whenever I came over here. I used to hate it, but they're our fans. I love them now. There'd be no Deep Purple without them and we have to be able to give them everything we've got."

Blackmore's behaviour at the California Jam probably made some stakeholders very angry and it is possible that it had an influence on how Deep Purple's performance was reviewed in the local press thereafter. In *The Los Angeles Times* in April 1974, in a feature article written after the California Jam (so bearing in mind that the article was reasonably extensive), all that was said of Deep Purple was that "Emerson, Lake & Palmer, which closed the show, clearly turned in the most dynamic set — a virtual feast of sights and sounds complete with fireworks. Deep Purple also offered a bit of flash, but its manner seemed more stilted."

Deep Purple played on the same stage that hosted Black Sabbath, who were at the heights of their success with *Sabbath*

*Bloody Sabbath* and Emerson, Lake & Palmer who were also doing tremendously well with their album, *Brain Salad Surgery*. The full line-up was: Rare Earth, Black Oak Arkansas, Seal & Croft, Earth, Wind & Fire, The Eagles, Black Sabbath, Deep Purple and Emerson, Lake & Palmer. This was very high-profile stuff indeed and Deep Purple were in the position of being able to demand $75,000 for their appearance. Lenny Stogel, one of the organisers of the California Jam, was quoted in *The Los Angeles Times* in April 1974; "It's going to be more than just a concert, it's going to be an event. We've done everything we can to assure a good show — staging, lighting, security, sound, talent, sanitary facilities, but it could be ruined by a single, stupid incident. That's our greatest fear now. Even a small incident could change the headlines from something like 200,000 kids have a marvellous time, to heaven knows what."

*The Springfield Leader & Press* reported in April 1974; "California Jam Festival Grosses Record $2 Million… Some 200,000 music fans thronged to the California Jam rock festival during the weekend for a concert that police said 'went off very well.' For the promoters, ABC Entertainment, the extravaganza may gross more money than any other concert of its kind. Similar events at Woodstock in 1969 and Watkins Glen last year, both in New York, drew larger crowds. However, gate crashers at Ontario Motor Speedway wasn't as much of a problem as it had been elsewhere, authorities said. At $10 a ticket, the advance price paid by more than 167,000 concert goers, and $15 paid at the gate by the rest, California Jam should gross about $2 million. The previous box office record was $1.5 million grossed by promoters of the Watkins Glen festival. Spokesmen for ABC Entertainment deferred comment on financial success until later in the week. Meanwhile today, police in this city forty miles east of LA said they were still trying to match up the last of the young concert goers with parents and the older fans with their automobiles. The concert started Saturday morning and wailed on into the night, but when it finally ended hundreds of fans found they couldn't leave. Their cars, parked illegally on the shoulder of Interstate 10 leading to the speedway, had been towed away. The pre-concert traffic jam — a monumental one stretching thirteen miles at one point — was the biggest problem of the event, which was generally peaceful. Ontario Police Sgt. George Cherry said 'there were a few isolated problems but for the number of people who were there, it went off really well'."

Precise arrest figures were not available but police estimated that between fifteen and twenty five were apprehended for investigation of offenses that included disturbing the peace, public intoxication, public nudity and possession of a deadly weapon. Only a few arrests were made on drug charges, though officers acknowledged that marijuana and some hard drugs were being used openly by many.

It was reported in *Melody Maker* in April 1974; "The promoters took in about two million dollars on the venture, but they didn't pocket a hell of a lot of money. The expenses to turn out what one critic called 'the aristocrat of rock concerts' were enormous."

Even as a relatively new band, Deep Purple Mk3 were taking things in their stride. When asked what the difficulties were of having joined such a high-profile band, Glenn Hughes was quoted in *Record World* in June 1976; "Obviously jumping on the bandwagon, jumping into the big time. I suppose it was an ego difficulty if you want to put it like that, but my ego isn't an out and out thing I like to show — my ego is only in my music. I thought there'd be no problem because my confidence in my music is very high, and there was no difficulty at all really. I was used to playing to large crowds, from being second on the bill on gigs with my old group (Trapeze) although I had not played at the big festivals like the California Jam or any of the outdoor football stadiums. They were different, I was playing to 60-70,000 people a night, which is a lot, but I just got into it."

By mid 1974, Deep Purple were going incredibly strong commercially. They had a reputation that could have plausibly seen them through the year without needing to make another album to stay at the top of their game. They had certainly made their mark with *Burn* and the tour that followed. Ultimately, if they felt strongly about taking some time off in the interest of rest and recuperation thereafter, to make such decision wouldn't have been unreasonable. For whatever reason though, it was decided, even while *Burn* was still sitting very comfortably on both the UK and US charts, that it was time to go back into the studio to make the next album, which had already been scheduled to be released before the year's end.

Even the record company themselves were well aware of the considerable speed at which Deep Purple were making albums. In Warner Bros.' *Circular* in November 1974, it was advocated of *Stormbringer*; "The additions of David Coverdale and bassist Glenn Hughes, *Burn*, the well publicised American tour on Starship One, the California Jam — it seems like the last Deep Purple barnstorming ended just a couple of weeks ago. Yet those prolific rogues are assaulting fall with still another burst of activity. A strong new LP, characteristically titled *Stormbringer*, has just been released. An international tour is already underway. Suffice to say Purple is back for more pillage with scarcely a moment's rest."

Understandably, this wasn't to Ritchie Blackmore's liking. He was quoted in *Modern Guitars* in 1975; "The main reason why I left Deep Purple is I didn't like the pressure from some of the record companies. We had signed a contract saying that we'd make three LPs a year and that just became too much for me. I come up with ideas once every two months or so, and I like to lay back for a year — make one good LP a year, which we were doing, if you follow Purple. To me, it was nonsense because we had no time to put it together. It was just strung together. *Machine Head* we had six weeks before, so it was a good LP. Then there was *Burn*, which was a good LP because we had six months before that. But the ones that came in between were thrown together and it was being dishonest to ourselves and the public. It was just like a product. It wasn't music anymore. The record company wanted a product on the market for kids to buy. Of course, the kids will buy it because they liked us on stage and liked the other LPs. But, in my opinion, they got a raw deal because they'd buy a good LP and then they'd buy a lot of padding. Then they'd be worried about the next LP, which was good instead of bad. And then the next LP after that was bad. I just wanted to lay back. One thing, in this business, it's a pity, but you've got to keep very consistent and musicians sometimes can't be consistent. To be creative, that doesn't mean you can be consistent all the time. You're searching for things. You try new songs. You can't just keep churning them out like a sausage factory. That's what we were becoming. And I didn't like it at all. A few of the other members were getting a bit fed up with it, too. I don't know if they've changed. I don't think they have because Purple songs will always have to sell a certain amount of records, whether I like it or not. There's nothing against Warner because we knew what we were signing when we signed it. But, it takes a couple of years to sink in. When you're touring, it becomes too much. And I wanted to get away from the high pressure of Deep Purple. So, getting away from the high pressure of turning out these bloody sausages to being in a band that is more in control, where we just put out music when we felt like it, that's what I'm trying to do now."

Fair comment. No matter how glamorous Deep Purple's touring commodities may have looked on the surface of things, everybody needs a holiday and like any job, if the holidays are crap, people don't always stick around. In that regard, it probably wouldn't be fair to think that Blackmore leaving to start his own band was an unreasonable move. Blackmore was quoted in *Rolling Stone* in April 1975; "We hardly ever rehearse together, except for a tour. When someone says we have to get an LP together, that's when we start pulling together songs. We're all very lazy, but professional enough to churn the songs out just in time. Deep Purple isn't too dedicated a band. I think we'd all rather sleep." In hindsight, there wasn't really anything lazy about needing a break after all that touring!

David Coverdale was quoted in *Record World* in June 1976; "*Stormbringer* suffered because we'd been working so long. Funnily enough Ritchie had said to me you probably won't be aware of the fact but we've been working so much when we finish this *Burn* album that by the next time we get a telephone call saying you're in the studio next week you won't have any material. So some of the stuff on *Stormbringer* would have been a lot better if we'd had a little more time to experiment."

With lots of things to be pissed off about, it makes sense that Blackmore could have been endeared to the more laid back style of working that support band Elf had. It comes across that, whilst Deep Purple were working incredibly hard as a by-product of being so in demand at that time, Elf were maybe having more fun. In May 1974, before the last show of the tour, record executives from all over the world attended a large event held in the ballroom at a Coventry hotel in order to present Deep Purple with all of the Gold and Platinum discs they had recently obtained. Elf's contribution to such party went on into the small hours whereby one Ronnie James Dio managed to self appoint himself as bartender for the night. The result was a very drunk band that included drummer Gary Driscoll dropping a fire extinguisher into a toilet bowl. It caused a breakage that released floods of water into the room underneath. It resulted in Elf being banned not only from the hotel, but the whole of

Coventry by the local police. The band were in trouble to the extent that, due to the public awareness of the incident, there was a risk that they could have been thrown off the tour and dropped by the record label. Everything worked out fine but their antics impressed Blackmore; his quirky sense of humour, penchant for practical jokes and ability to have at least some influence on management was such that ultimately, it all went in Elf's favour and certainly, Dio's.

Blackmore was quoted in *Modern Guitars* in 1975; "There's a community thing. We understand each other's humour, each other's jokes. And basically the guys are quiet. I'm quiet, maybe moody. With Purple, they had a different sense of humour than what I liked. I was more into the practical jokes, a very dry sense of humour. They were more into verbal, witty jokes, and you'd be surprised how that can destroy a relationship in a way because I never laughed when they did and vice versa. Also, I think I got to a stage where I was thinking, 'I still haven't proved myself yet. I still want to be more and more and more' but I got the impression sometimes that they were quite happy to sit back and let things ride a bit. And I never got very much emotion out of Deep Purple music, though I did when I was onstage. Except for *Machine Head* and *In Rock*, there wasn't a lot that moved me about what we did and I could never figure out why. It was just misinterpretation between the guitar and the vocalist most of the time, which wasn't their fault. I just had a very bad way of explaining myself, of what I wanted put over the top. Plus, it got to the stage where I couldn't really say, I couldn't tell a singer what to sing. I didn't want to. He's the singer. He should sing whatever he feels. That's why it's different in this band (Rainbow). Everybody's thinking together. Nobody's got big egos."

With still being relatively new to an intensively busy life on the road, Coverdale and Hughes opted to spend their spare time working with Jon Lord. This included, on 1st June

1974 in Munich, staging some classical and rock fusion at the Eurovision presentation of Prix Jeunesse. *Continuo On BACH* and *Windows* both built upon Lord's interest in fusing classical music with rock, as he had done previously with his *Gemini Suite* and prior to that with all of Mk2 Deep Purple, *Concerto For Group And Orchestra*.

Commercially, Lord's work outside of Deep Purple didn't reach tremendous heights but the fact is, he never lost interest in classical music and it comes across that it was something he needed to do either way. Certainly, it was a huge part of his musical career outside of Deep Purple and indeed, was the genre of music in which he had initially trained when taking formal piano examinations.

As with a lot of classical music, it either grabs people or it doesn't. *Windows* was reviewed by *Record Mirror* in August 1974; "So here we have the Deep Purple keyboards wizard, Jon Lord, the talented Tony Ashton, David Coverdale, Ray Fenwick, Glenn Hughes and Pete York, the Orchestra of the Munich Chamber Opera conducted by Eberhard Schoener who composed all the music with Lord, and yet somehow they don't seem to have got it really together. Side one is *Continuo On BACH*, a realisation of a well known incomplete fugue by Bach, and 'Window' on side two is based on a form of chain poetry called Renga which was developed in the Far East in the fourteenth Century. I can but criticise these works from a humble position since my musical knowledge is no match with the composers. This album takes a lot of listening and it didn't particularly grab me. No doubt many will hail it as brilliant."

**Purple album details**

DEEP PURPLE'S new album is titled "Stormbringer" and will be released simultaneously around the world on November 1. The tracks on the album are, Side One: "Stormbringer", "Love Don't Mean A Thing", "Holy Man", "Hold On"; Side Two: "Lady Double Dealer", "You Can't Do It Right", "Highball Shooter", "The Gypsy", "Soldier Of Fortune.

# sounds

MUSIC IS THE MESSAGE

NOVEMBER 2, 1974  10p

THIS WEEK IN
THE 'SOUNDS COLLECTION
**FULL COLOUR POSTER OF**
SEE CENTRE PAGES
**ROD STEWART**

## DEEP PURPLE — IN FROM THE RAIN
Lead singer Dave Coverdale talks about the new album "Stormbringer"

**McCartney: new Wings**

**Rock and roll Winter**

**Jack the Bruce's back**

**The Spector spectre laid**

**Szymczyk's the name**

*Harley: mr soft gets tough*

# Chapter Three

## The Making Of Stormbringer

Whilst Jon Lord had a constructive outlet for his musical interests outside of Deep Purple, Blackmore, Hughes and Coverdale had all expressed interests at various points in a number of interviews that individually, they wanted to do projects outside of Deep Purple as a vehicle to better support their personal music interests outside of the restrictions and expectations of the group.

In some ways, it could be considered that *Stormbringer* is a culmination of musicians all pulling in different directions. It is an extremely varied album stylistically and it is no secret that individual band members had significantly conflicting ideas about what should (and indeed shouldn't) be on the album. The end result was that in some ways, *Stormbringer* was something of a compromise and it was evident that this was the case even when promotional interviews for the album were taking place.

Blackmore was quoted in Warner Bros.' November 1974 *Circular*; "Glenn is heavily into R&B. He lives for funky music. So it obviously creeps in from his side. Funk doesn't really turn me on. As long as it's got melody it's okay, but I prefer the heavy metal things. We can handle funk though — we do it quite well. I just don't particularly like that stuff too much. The real out-and-out funk, it's very monotonous. I think we've managed to keep the melody and heavy rock influence without losing out to an endless James Brown soul riff."

In the same feature, Blackmore was quoted as having

said something that, in hindsight, suggests that by the time of promoting *Stormbringer*, he was probably just going through the motions and yet, in fairness, the professionalism was still there. When asked how he would compare *Stormbringer* to *Burn*, Blackmore was quoted; "Amazingly enough, I like them both. I'm trying to think of the songs on *Burn*. I like the song 'Burn' itself. 'Sail Away', I thought was great. I suppose there are a few more good tracks on the new album. For once though, I think we've got two good albums out in a row. It's usually up and down. *In Rock* was good, but *Fireball* was terrible. *Machine Head* was very good, then we went down with *Who Do We Think We Are*. Not counting *Made In Japan*, which was all right I guess, we went up again with *Burn*. I thought more than likely this would be a downer. So I'm happy about everything. I was a bit worried because as a band we don't rehearse much. We hardly ever rehearse at all to be honest. We're very lazy. We tend to sleep a lot, watch television — do anything but write songs. But when someone says we've got to get an album together, at least we're professional enough to work very quickly. And we churn a record out. We're not too dedicated as a band, but I think as individual players we probably are. Getting together is always a bit of a struggle. Getting Jon out of bed and me to the gig. Always trouble."

Further to this, Blackmore's rejected ideas saw the light of day on the 1975 *Ritchie Blackmore's Rainbow* album and ideas of the others that didn't make it to *Stormbringer* were carried forward onto Deep Purple's next album, *Come Taste The Band* (also in 1975), with Tommy Bolin taking Blackmore's place on guitar.

Glenn Hughes was quoted in *Record World* in June 1976; "The first one I did, *Burn*, was a little too broad, it was too basic rock for me, and the next one, *Stormbringer*, was the least productive but I liked doing it, but I have to say that *Come Taste The Band* was the best album for me to play and sing on."

David Coverdale was quoted in the same feature; "A lot of the songs I've taken to Purple could have been rearranged and done by anybody but when you give a piece to Ian Paice or Ritchie Blackmore or Jon Lord they put their stamp on it, which inevitably comes out as Purple. It's as good as the conception I had before but I want to experiment now with a little more subtlety."

By the mid seventies, the independent music press was a powerful aspect of the media to the extent that perhaps some of what was written exacerbated the tensions that were present within Deep Purple at the time. Throughout August 1974, a fair bit of attention was paid to the fact that Deep Purple were working on the album that came to be known as *Stormbringer*. The pressure might have really been on to deliver the goods in terms of musical quality.

Ironically, things could have been pretty comfortable financially. The band was doing well in that regard but sadly, this is perhaps where egos come into play. With *Burn*, Blackmore had put the idea forward that, unlike the shared writing credits system that Mk2 used, Mk3 band members would only be credited for the songs that they were actively involved in the composition of. The Mk3 way of doing things probably added an element of creative risk to both *Burn* and *Stormbringer* due to the fact that it could have resulted in individual musicians wanting to push for getting their particular ideas on the albums, purely for reasons that perhaps related to ego, status and money. Of course, there's no way of telling what motivates each individual human being, but would the Mk3 way of crediting things have opened the door to at least some sense of awkwardness? Absolutely!

Time had been set aside for Deep Purple to work on *Stormbringer* in June and July 1974. On the surface of things, this sounds advantageous considering that many of the band's earlier albums were made alongside a heavy touring schedule.

However, due to the fact that Mk3 weren't spending a lot of time together socially by this point and had just completed a busy tour, the motivation to prepare for the album prior to going into the studio was minimal. Upon being asked whether he was pleased with *Burn* and *Stormbringer*, Blackmore was quoted in *Sounds* in February 1975; "Yeah, they're okay. I'm never pleased with anything really. We had a couple of months' rehearsal before each of those albums. Unfortunately at those rehearsals we were booked into this castle in Wales where Bad Company and Joe Cocker rehearse and we just played football and had séances all the time. That's all we did, nobody ever bloody did anything. It was terrible. It was like everybody was so lazy, Jon wouldn't get up until about six at night, come straight down for a meal, stay there until about ten o'clock at night and go down to the studio and by that time I'd got pissed off anyway and I had to go to bed. So we hardly saw each other. And then we suddenly realised we only had about four days left until we went into the studio so we all went, 'Uh, what are we gonna play, what are we gonna play?'."

David Coverdale was quoted in Martin Popoff's 2015 book, *Sail Away*; "*Stormbringer* was written mostly in the studio which was a huge expense, very time consuming and you kept having to compromise just in order to get it done." *Stormbringer* was Deep Purple's first album to be recorded in a studio environment since *Fireball*.

Musicland Studios was established by Italian record producer, songwriter and performer Giorgio Moroder in the late 1960s. Situated in the basement of the Arabellahaus Hotel. Deep Purple was one of the first of the major British acts to use it, but Musicland would go on to become a popular choice for many artists, including Queen, The Rolling Stones, Led Zeppelin, Electric Light Orchestra and many more. Producer Martin Birch thought highly of it and equally, it was used for Deep Purple and Rainbow albums thereafter.

## The Making Of Stormbringer

Much to Blackmore's frustration, where his ideas for riff-oriented rock with plenty of virtuoso soloing opportunities were once welcomed, during the recording of *Stormbringer*, planned solos and established song structures had been worked out in advance. Blackmore was quoted of the structure of the songs on *Stormbringer* in *Circus Raves* in January 1975; "There's not so much improvisation going on. We've cut down on that. We realised that most of our songs consist of two verses, guitar solo, organ solo, verse, middle eight, and then another solo and it all gets a bit boring. It's more of a tune album, with nine songs."

Whilst such a way of working provided scope for accuracy and precision, it did not lend itself to the same extent of emotional interpretation of the music that, throughout his career, Blackmore has become well known for. He was quoted in *Modern Guitars* in 1975; "Two tracks on *Stormbringer* were so hard to put together just because certain people in the band wanted to play funk. It was a real hardship to get across to them, 'let's just put a melody down. We're not gonna have the kind of brilliant solos from anybody' you know, kind of, what's the word? Virtuoso kind of parts, no organ solos, just a good song. But it was always the old story of, 'there must be an organ solo, a guitar solo, drum beat must be pretty good and this and that' which detracted from a good song. One song I'm thinking of in particular, 'Soldier Of Fortune', I really had to twist a couple of the band's arms to kind of get the song down, which is one of my favourites. But because it's so laid back and it's very melodic and there's not a lot of funk there, it was getting to the point where I thought, you know, we're moving apart."

Such was Blackmore's disinterest in *Stormbringer* overall that he couldn't remember every song on the album by name. Blackmore was quoted of a track on *Stormbringer* that he didn't like in *Circus Raves* in January 1975; "I wrote the progression, unfortunately. Although the vocals stand up well, the content of the music on this particular track isn't so hot. I didn't stick around to find out the title of the tune even, although I recall it's in the key of A". (Based on the *Stormbringer* sheet music published by Warner Bros in 1975, I advocate that it is most likely that Blackmore was referring to 'High Ball Shooter').

With Ian Paice not needing to be so involved with the debates surrounding melodic decisions, 'High Ball Shooter' begins with a strong and tightly played rhythm. The song was the third from *Stormbringer* to be used in Mk3's live sets.

Upon initial assessment, it would be easy to conclude that Blackmore's comment was indicative of a lack of engagement in the making of *Stormbringer*. However, he was quoted in the same feature in a way that puts it down to the way that *Stormbringer*'s recording was scheduled; "That's the trouble with having an allotted time to make an album — you invariably miss out on one or two tracks. We rehearsed in a castle in Wales for two or three weeks but we had more séances and games of football than we actually rehearsed. We recorded it in Munich, Germany, in three weeks, with Martin Birch, our engineer, who's now doing our stage sound as well."

Still though, once he had left Deep Purple, Blackmore was probably in a better position to be more candid about his feelings on *Stormbringer*. He was quoted of it in *Modern Guitars* in 1975; "There was one track on the album I despise. I forget what it's even called. It was a track they always picked up on the radio. They played it all the bloody time. It's a typical rock 'n' roll nothing. We wrote it on the spot. I don't even know what it's called. Doesn't matter."

Coverdale was quoted in *Sounds* in November 1974 as he explained that by the time of recording *Stormbringer*, he and Hughes were very strongly encouraged by the rest of the band to make executive decisions about the music; "They were turning round and asking our opinions because they needed a refreshing course, they wanted to know what our ideas were and we told them. It took Glenn and I a while to get used to the idea of telling people of their musical stature what to do. It was difficult on *Burn* to get the gumption together but now like, the new album for me is such a mature logical progression. On *Burn* we didn't know each other, I'm not ashamed of the album by any means but we were still getting to know each other."

Unusually for his time in Deep Purple up to that point, Blackmore wasn't given a writing credit on some of the *Stormbringer* songs; 'Holy Man' and 'Hold On'. But in fairness, can a musician be credited for having a written a song when they were, at least predominantly, absent from the process?

Glenn Hughes stated in his 2017 edition autobiography that when they went into the studio to record *Stormbringer*; "We hardly had any songs completed. The only one that Ritchie had come close to finishing was 'Stormbringer'. The rest of it was pretty much written around David, myself and Jon. 'Holy Man' was written around the piano for sure."

Blackmore later put his lack of engagement with *Stormbringer* down to the personal problems he was having at the time; his marriage of six years was at breaking point and personally, his focus was elsewhere. Blackmore was quoted in *Sounds* in February 1975; "On *Stormbringer* there wasn't as much guitar because I was in a way going through more personal problems. I was thinking about other things when I should have been thinking about music. I didn't have the people there that I wanted to have there." Still though, there was no denying the fact that in his career at least, his eyes were on a different prize in the form of his work outside of Deep Purple.

It was reported in *Circus Raves* in January 1975; "One of the first storms they came across in recording their latest album was a song that everyone in the group seemed to like — except Ritchie. Called 'Hold On', it flowed from the pen of Jon Lord as a shuffle progression with Ritchie playing a blues solo. The amount of effort Ritchie put into it was not up to the level of the other tracks, so the rest of the band had to push even harder."

Blackmore was quoted in the same feature; "I like going from one extreme to the other — very hard music and classical pretty music like Bach — and I don't like anything in between. A lot of people like that track, but it isn't really one of my favourites."

There is an interesting point to be made about whether or not David Coverdale and Glenn Hughes had a good working relationship whilst working on *Stormbringer*. On the one hand, it comes across that Hughes really wanted to be a singer, much more so than a bass player. Glenn Hughes was quoted in *Disc* in May 1974; "I wouldn't have even joined the bleedin' Beatles as just a bass player. I wouldn't have joined any band where I couldn't be guaranteed at least fifty per cent of the singing. I liked Purple and they wanted a new style. What's more, they wanted two singers, so when it was suggested I join them, I thought carefully and decided to do it. Although I was really into Trapeze and their music — I think they're one of the most underrated bands in the country — I couldn't see a way I'd ever make it with them. So I joined Deep Purple. At first, when we were rehearsing for *Burn*, I wasn't too happy, although I wouldn't tell the rest of the band. You see I thought I wasn't going to be singing enough. But the way it worked out I'm doing quite a lot so everything is fine."

It could be considered that Hughes had some frustrations due to Coverdale being the lead singer. When asked if he saw himself as more of a vocalist or bass player, Glenn Hughes was quoted in *Record World* in June 1976; "I'd have to say definitely a vocalist. I used to play guitar before bass in the early Trapeze and moved on to bass, and I've been playing a piano for the last eighteen months, which I really enjoy. Obviously I'm a singer and I think of this as being most important. I don't want to shove Dave (Coverdale) off, obviously, because he's the lead singer, but the band realises I'm a singer. That's another reason why I have to do my solo album, I just love singing."

Hughes was quoted in *Sounds* in November 1975; "In Trapeze we were playing rock 'n' soul, and I'm now starting on a solo album which is being produced by David Bowie and features people like Herbie Hancock, Dennis Davis, Tommy Bolin, Dave Sanborn and Ava Cherry and her singers." It wasn't to be though. Hughes stated in his 2017 edition autobiography; "I was unsure of what Purple were going to be without Ritchie. I knew that David and I were becoming the main song writers, and I was also gearing up to do my own album, but I was too fucked up to do that and didn't have the balls." (Hughes was presented with a number of opportunities based on his friendship with David Bowie at the time of making *Stormbringer*. Such opportunities were rumoured to include a super session featuring (as was reported in *Sounds* in March 1975) "Jagger, Richards, John Entwistle, Jim Keltner and the Memphis Horns." But as Hughes was quoted in the same feature; "I can't do it due to my commitments with Purple, but it was nice getting the offer.").

Hughes himself has stipulated that he and Coverdale had a good working relationship, so much so that they did a lot of the writing together on *Stormbringer* while the rest of Deep Purple were otherwise occupied. Glenn Hughes stated in his autobiography; "When we were in Musicland in Germany in 1974 making *Stormbringer*, we had to get out of there because the Rolling Stones were coming in to use the studio, so most of the vocals were done at the Record Plant in LA. We were also two songs short, hence 'High Ball Shooter' and 'The Gypsy'. But we hadn't sung 'Hold On' and we hadn't sung 'You Can't Do It Right'. So Blackmore was gone and it was basically just me and David."

In his book, Hughes also said of 'Holy Man'; "I just love this song. It was agreed that I would do a song on my own and David and I came up with the chords one night in the studio."

And of 'Soldier Of Fortune'; "David was in his element here. I like to hear David singing in this register, he has a wonderful tone."

'Holy Man' was the first Deep Purple song not to credit Blackmore as a writer since 'Chasing Shadows' and 'Blind' on the band's eponymous album made with the Mk1 line-up in 1969. Hughes asserted in later years that the song is about being on the road and asking for the spiritual strength to keep at it, even when times are tough. Despite Blackmore not being credited as a writer on 'Holy Man', his innovative approach was still present as a musician. Hughes recalled how Blackmore didn't want anyone to be in the room while he recorded his solo but made an exception for Glenn. Hughes suggested that Blackmore played the solo with a slide and due to a random screwdriver being within closer reaching distance, Blackmore opted to use that and got the solo down in one take.

Upon being asked whether all of Mk3's songs were collaborations, Blackmore was quoted in *Sounds* in February 1975; "No they're not and if you look on the new album (*Stormbringer*) you'll see everybody isn't credited. I write with Dave (Coverdale) because he always writes the lyrics, I don't like to write lyrics. I do but it would be kind of like a session singer, here's the lyrics, here's the backing, here's the song, and he doesn't do anything. I like him to work out his own lyrics, the way he feels, and I come up with chord progressions and riffs but they always alter them just slightly to their own taste."

'Hold On' grew from an idea that Jon Lord came up with and Coverdale considered that whilst Blackmore wasn't keen on the idea, he still played well on the solo, even though there was a sense that he couldn't really be bothered with it. It is the story of legend that this was the case to the extent that in an act of defiance, Blackmore claimed that he played the entire solo with his thumb (I say that this is the stuff of legend because in the mid nineties when Blackmore asked vocalist Doogie White to join Rainbow, White wasn't convinced that it was Blackmore on the phone and in order to check the validity of the caller's identity, White asked the man who claimed to be Blackmore some questions about this guitar solo on *Stormbringer*).

'Hold On' was never played live but David Bowie thought highly enough of the track that he considered doing a cover of it. Coverdale was quoted of *Stormbringer* in *Sounds* in November 1974; "I can see other artists covering material on this album while there are not many other Purple songs that you can imagine being covered. There are several people that have expressed interest at certain tunes on the album, Bowie wants to do one. It sounds typical recording artist bullshit but I'm just looking forward to the next one, y'know, the progression thing."

Blackmore was quoted of *Stormbringer* in *Circus Raves* in January 1975; "The album is even more funky than *Burn*, although I'm not too hung up on funky music. I'm for pretty music, or hard rock. Funk can tend to get a bit tedious, though it's great to dance to. But there's one track on the new album called 'Money' (Actually 'Love Don't Mean A Thing'), it was written by a guy we met on the road, some coloured guy who came up to me at a party and said 'hey man, I got a song for you' so I said right, leave me alone, but he insisted and so I told him to sing it. So he started snapping his fingers and singing it, and it sounds great. I figured if it sounds that good with just him snapping his fingers, it'd be a good tune for the band. We rearranged it, added some parts. It's the first time in six years that we've accepted a song from somebody else."

Blackmore wrote the riff for 'Lady Double Dealer'. This isn't particularly surprising considering the overall heavy rock style of the song. Glenn Hughes stated of it in his 2017 edition autobiography; "A straightforward Blackmore song. It was just straight rock. It was okay." In terms of the completed track, Blackmore wasn't too pleased with it. He was quoted of 'Lady

Double Dealer' in *Modern Guitars* in 1975; "I think it came out too clean. It was more of a rock 'n' roll song. It should be rough and edgy. It should be more distorted and I think the vocal was too outstanding. It was too up front."

Blackmore's use of medieval influences is evident on 'Soldier Of Fortune', particularly in the song's use of chords. Effectively, they add a sense of melancholy to the melody and the same applies on 'The Gypsy'. It is very similar to what was achieved with 'Sixteenth Century Greensleeves' on *Ritchie Blackmore's Rainbow*. Still though, it's a bit of a shame that for 'Soldier Of Fortune', Blackmore had to negotiate with the rest of the band to be able to put the track on *Stormbringer*. That can't have been a nice feeling.

That said, Coverdale was on Blackmore's side. According to Coverdale they wrote the song together at Clearwell Castle while the rest of the band were playing soccer. Also, as much as there is a strong narrative that Coverdale predominantly wanted to refer to funk and soul influences for making *Stormbringer*, it was the case that Coverdale shared some of Blackmore's musical interests in the form of Bach, English folk music and early Jethro Tull. Whilst *Stormbringer* was the last time that Coverdale and Blackmore would work together in the studio, the sad thing perhaps is that plausibly, there would have been a time when the two of them worked effectively together, at least from a creative perspective.

Coverdale was quoted in Martin Popoff's 2015 book, *Sail Away*; "'Lay Down, Stay Down' (on *Burn*) was one of the first lyrics I wrote. It was interesting. Obviously I was in awe (of Blackmore), my whole inspiration was Hendrix, that style of guitar playing. And Blackmore was a phenomenal musician. I'd always worked with good players but these guys were something else and, of course, they had the ego and the sound equipment to put their money where their mouth was. So working with Ritchie was a marriage made in heaven.

And I was learning as I was going. I'm a good sponge and I was soaking it all in. And the more comfortable I felt, the more comfortable I felt providing musical ideas. Because I had been writing for a few years, just with the local bands. And we connected very well. Both of us were fans of medieval music, which is a modal concept similar to Bach, and we both enjoyed similar acts or whatever, and so I would feel more comfortable putting in chord ideas and melodies."

When it came to the mixing stage of making *Stormbringer*, Blackmore put in minimal appearances but having had a lot of his ideas so explicitly rejected by the rest of the band by that point, who can blame him.

Martin Birch considered that Blackmore had lost interest completely by the time it came to mixing *Stormbringer* (when asked about his experiences of producing *Come Taste The Band*, Martin Birch was quoted in *Record World* in June 1976; "The absence of Ritchie was obvious. It was almost obvious on *Stormbringer*. They'd been together a long time then. Musical differences started on *Stormbringer* and after that Ritchie decided that he wanted to go his own way.").

Glenn Hughes stated in his autobiography; "Although we recorded *Stormbringer* in August 1974, there was barely any communication between the band and Ritchie by the end of the year. There'd never been much anyway. If he wasn't happy about something, he'd send a roadie to us with a note. But I knew what kind of guy he was before I got in the band. When Jon had a couple of drinks he became the David Niven of rock, doing card tricks and telling stories and being great company. Ian was more isolated, and Ritchie was out on his own most of the time, so apart from Coverdale and me it really wasn't a band of pals — which was unusual because I'd come from Trapeze, who were all close friends."

Warner Bros.' November 1974 *Circular* reported of Blackmore; "It was the morning after *Stormbringer*'s final LA mixing session when we spoke with lead guitarist and founding member, Ritchie Blackmore. The weary Blackmore, always refreshingly cynical, proved in fine self-deprecating form." Blackmore was then quoted in the same feature; 'I spend so much time making the fucking albums, I get pissed off with talking about them. Especially when I get asked about the words because I have nothing to do with lyrics. So don't ask me what they're about 'cause I don't have the slightest.' When asked if he thought Deep Purple listeners pay attention to the lyrics, Blackmore's response was, "I don't know. I don't listen to Deep Purple."

One of the earlier suggestions for the cover art of *Stormbringer* was a photograph of some post-riot damage from fans at a concert in Japan. It was eventually decided that this wasn't a good idea on the basis that it wasn't the message that Deep Purple wanted to put out there about their music and their fans. The photograph chosen for the album art is that of a tornado. The image had been used before on Miles Davis' 1970 album, *Bitches Brew*. The original monochrome photograph was taken by Lucille Handberg on 8th July 1927 in Minnesota and then the mythical creature and the colours in the sky were edited on top of the famous image. The duty of doing the cover for *Stormbringer* was given to John Cabalka and it was he who commissioned artist Joe Garnett to paint on top of the photo, using oil paints to achieve the desired effect. Between them, both Cabalka and Garnett have extensive credits for their work on album covers. Cabalka created more than one hundred and seventy-five album covers. Garnett worked on album covers for Captain Beyond, Jethro Tull, REO Speedwagon and Cheech & Chong.

By November 1974, sharing the bill with Electric Light Orchestra and Elf, Deep Purple started their next tour of America. With Blackmore's rapport with Deep Purple being so fragmented, he found himself associating more with Elf's

## The Making Of Stormbringer

lead singer Ronnie James Dio. The more they talked, the more they found that they had a lot of musical interests in common and it was on the road that Dio had started writing what would become Rainbow's song, 'Sixteenth Century Greensleeves'. Blackmore liked the song to the extent that he was keen to get it down as the B-side for a planned single release of 'Black Sheep Of The Family' that had been recorded by Quatermass in 1970. Studio time was booked for them in Tampa Bay for the 12th December. Also on the session was the rest of Elf and ELO cellist Hugh McDowell. Happy with the way things were developing Blackmore and Dio soon had an album's worth of songs that they were keen to record.

Deep Purple's touring commitments weren't too time consuming at the beginning of 1975. There was a solitary gig at the Sunbury Festival — Australia's answer to Woodstock — on the 25th January. Being invited to play at the gig was, like with the California Jam, certainly demonstrative of Deep Purple's supergroup status at the time but ultimately, the Sunbury Festival was a bit of a washout due to the weather.

In the context of expressing his reservations about *Stormbringer*, Blackmore was quoted in *Circus Raves* in January 1975; "Every other artist probably has this problem — you tend to put out a little bit of junk. Three quarters of an album is the most you can hope for, unless you're someone like McCartney and Stevie Wonder, both of whom usually put out one hundred per cent good music. Whether you tend to like the type of music they do or not, they seem to have so much music in them they can just turn it out, whereas with our band we have to work at it. A lot of it comes at the last stages when Deep Purple is making an album — when we realise that we've got to make an album and finish it, and we don't have much time left. It's quite demanding. You have to have nine songs, and they've got to be good or there's no point in making them. I don't know whether I could play someone else's songs, unless someone like McCartney was writing them. In fact, we might ask him to write something for us in the future 'cause he's a genius. Another group that writes very good singles and is underestimated is Badfinger, they write really lovely singles."

It was reported in *Melody Maker* in February 1975; "Blackmore has recently been practicing the cello in a beach house up near Ventura Beach (just north of LA). Ritchie has a solo project on his mind at the moment and while in one city on this past tour, he booked time in a studio to lay down some tracks for a single he'll be hoping to release on his own. Other solo aspirations or interests the boys have outside of the band are generally more out in the open. Glenn and David Bowie share a common affinity for black music and through that, he explained, 'me and David have before very close friends (sic). I've been staying with him in New York and we're going to do an album next year, the two of us'."

There was a time limit on how long Blackmore could spend on his work outside of Deep Purple. After Elf's *Trying To Burn The Sun* album was released, in mid-February Blackmore flew Dio, Mickey Lee Soule, Gary Driscoll, and Craig Gruber to Musicland Studios in Munich to work on what would become the first Rainbow album. Blackmore's girlfriend at the time, Shoshana, contributed backing vocals on 'Catch The Rainbow' and 'Still I'm Sad'.

The album was completed on 14th March, just two days before Deep Purple's European tour was due to start in Yugoslavia on 16th, making the most of the available studio time that had initially been booked by Deep Purple for the follow up to *Stormbringer*, which Purple had decided to put back until after the planned European tour was completed in April.

But with Blackmore leaving Purple after the last show in Paris on 7th April, he was quoted in *Modern Guitars* in 1975 on his new venture; "It's not my band. It's a band that I got together with Ronnie. I put my name to the first LP as being *Ritchie Blackmore's Rainbow* to get people to know that I've left Deep Purple. More to kind of say, 'If you like that kind of music, this is where I'm at' — I hope to drop that later because I couldn't handle the responsibility of doing all the interviews and all that bullshit, which I'm doing now, that goes with having your own group. Plus, I don't want to have my own group. This group, they're so good. You know, I'm part of the group. It's not me and the group, no way. I don't want to have that scene at all... It's definitely a new band, same as like Purple was. It's not me and the band. To start, I don't consider myself that good to front the band and I don't want to front the band. I'll only do my flash business on stage, which I like doing. But I just don't like being known as a leader of the band. I'd like to be a pusher, obviously, of the band. Nobody can be a leader of a band if they're really truthful. And if you're someone like Rory Gallagher, well Rory's good, but everybody else is his side band, kind of playing to back him up — this is not that kind of band. With Rainbow, they're all stars in their own right, especially the singer. He'll prove himself, you know. But at first, it's gonna be slanted my way because of being with Purple. But it's good in a way because people will take a listen to what else we've got to offer, whereas maybe if we were a completely unknown band, they wouldn't take time."

The speed at which Rainbow's debut album was made was not to its disadvantage. Released in August 1975, it got to number thirty in America and to number eleven in the UK where it went Silver. Commercially, it was Blackmore's most successful record after *Machine Head*. It was in June 1975 that Blackmore's departure from Deep Purple was officially announced in *Sounds*.

In an interview with *Metal Express Radio* in May 2008, Jon Lord said; "We had a really good change when David and Glenn came in and we did a really good album in *Burn* and I thought it carried on with the Deep Purple tradition very well. David and Glenn certainly did have more of an influence on *Stormbringer* for the simple reason that Ritchie took his eye off the ball as he had his idea in his head about Rainbow and he didn't feel that David and Glenn were the right kind of people to carry that side of him forward and then he decided to leave. He could've been stronger during the making of *Stormbringer* and if he had been stronger then *Stormbringer* could have been a better album, not that it's a bad album but it could've been a better one. It's quite a confusing album. At the time our fans got a little confused by it. With *Burn* we picked up the torch and ran with it, I just wish we could have stayed with it. I think Ritchie lost a bit of energy trying to deal with the runaway train that was Glenn Hughes. It's well documented that Glenn has had his drug and alcohol problems and thank goodness he's sorted those out now, but at the time he was a bit of a loose cannon and hard to deal with and I think Ritchie had just had enough."

# Deep Purple
## STORMBRINGER

Album TPS 3508
Cassette TC-TPS 3508
Cartridge 8X-TPS 3508

Deep Purple - Stormbringer: In-depth

# Chapter Four

## Mk3 As A Live Band

Ritchie Blackmore was quoted in *Circus* in September 1975; "I think *Stormbringer* was alright, but Purple's always been best onstage, and you know me, I'm never happy with my music." When asked if he ever got tired playing in Deep Purple, he was quoted in *Sounds* in February 1975; "On record, yeah, on stage no. On stage I just show off and play what I want to play. It looks better on stage because you can show off a bit, improvise, play what you want. But it's really not good to take much notice of what I say because I'm never really that excited about anything." On being happier with Mk3 onstage rather than in the studio, the guitarist was quoted in *Disc* in August 1975; "I think it was *Stormbringer* ironically which brought matters to a head. That was almost impossible to record — I hated it. And then when they wanted to start recording again it was the last straw. On stage they were great, but Purple in the studio could never really come up to the same standard."

As a live band, the story of Deep Purple Mk3 is one that went from strength to strength. Ian Paice was quoted in *Sounds* in December 1973 as he advocated of one of the early Mk3 live shows; "The excitement was there but the music wasn't that together. No one has seen the real potential of this band, I think we'll be bigger than we've been before." He wasn't wrong. This was just the beginning of things for Mk3 Deep Purple as a live band.

Coverdale was quoted in *Sounds* in November 1974 as he described his first gig with Deep Purple; "The first gig was in Copenhagen and the band thought I had shit out y'know, they thought that I had got so nervous that I'd pissed off because there were loads of press around and the usual backstage hassle and before I had always been on my own with the band. But this was all so new y'know all the shit that goes with it and I could see that everybody was as nervous as I was. I went upstairs to a room on my own and I sat there and had a little discussion with myself, either I would go out there and fall flat on my face or I'd go out there and do it. Then I came down and saw so many doubtful faces looking at me thinking 'what's he gonna do, he's nowt special' and I thought 'that does it, I'll show the bastards!' — and that was the whole thing I went on with the intention of showing them and it worked."

Regarding the fact that Ian Gillan had quite the stronghold on Deep Purple's audiences, Coverdale was quoted in the same feature; "To be quite honest I never considered it. I never considered myself as a replacement, it was a new thing. As far as they were concerned it was a new band. They just had a reputation to live up to and an excellent one at that."

With *Burn* having successfully provided Mk3 Deep Purple with a dynamic setlist and with their tour schedule having been organised well, the ingredients were there for the band to get through to audiences in the live arena. Coverdale was quoted in *Record World* in June 1976; "After my first six months with the band, which covered most of the European tours and American tours, (Jon Lord) complimented me on the fact that there'd been no calls for Ian (Gillan) from the audience. This isn't knocking Ian at all — I think we just came up with the goods at the time. We proved that it was a fine transition. My voice isn't anything like Ian's, and I've since met Ian and we get on famously. It's like a mutual admiration society. I've heard his new album and I love it. It's very much like a feather in my cap, I don't think people stopped thinking about Ian Gillan at all, it was like 'Oh he's alright as well'."

The exuberance of the performances at the California Jam was certainly explicit but it was probably done with a sense of gusto. Jon Lord was quoted of the California Jam in *New Musical Express* in April 1974; "Both ELP and ourselves have had the same sort of criticism at one time or another. You know, over-loud, over-indulgent. But if it worries them as much as it worries us, they can't be very bothered. As it happens I like what Keith (Emerson) does very much. We got the opportunity to choose when we'd go on and we chose sunset. ELP went on last, during the dark. But it even got down to quibbling about whose name was to go on the left side of the poster because, apparently, that's the most prominent spot in the natural line of vision. Ours did, as a matter of fact."

Deep Purple were still flying high and wowing audiences just a few days after the California Jam. As was reported in *New Musical Express* in April 1974; "America for Deep Purple is a huge success story, and getting bigger. Out front there are another 18,000 kids waiting for them — and it's their third gig in the Los Angeles area in four days… Purple hit the stage and are straight into a heavy instrumental jam. Purple have now completely surpassed The Faces in Stateside popularity. The California Jam, which they played two days before, drawing a quarter of a million people, had grossed two million dollars. 'This is the last gig of our tour,' hollers David Coverdale, 'So it's gonna be a blast-aah!' They take straight off into 'Burn'. 'Gonna give you ta Mista Lord,' announces Blackmore (sic). Lord and Paice take over the next two numbers, Paice's drums turning blue, pink and purple, while Lord throws his organ through the most excruciating gyrations — 'I wan' you so badleee,' screams Coverdale. Blackmore's guitar is now twelve feet in the air, now crashed down against the stage, and seven-eighths smashed before a roadie runs on with a replacement for the final riffs. Then they're away, gone. Of course they'll get called back for an encore, but the audience has to wait over six minutes — until, right on a screaming crescendo, they're back. 'More! More! More!' There's to be a party aboard the Starship tonight, to finish off all the un-drunk champagne and to say goodbye to the roadies. None of the band are given to any hype about how big they are, although they're well aware of how successful they're becoming, and how unique among British bands in having cracked the American market first go. They are all more than enthusiastic about their next US tour (in August) for which they'll be hiring the Starship again if they can get it. But for now it's all eyes on the road for their British tour. Apparently they've sold out the Hammersmith Odeon in a record seven minutes. No wonder, as it's been a long time since Britain got a look at this home-grown billion-dollar proposition."

Whilst today, it would be very unfair to negate the merits of what Gillan and Glover brought to the band during the Mk2 days, by April 1974, Mk3 Deep Purple was a tightly run unit and the band seemed to be working well together. As was reported in *New Musical Express* in April 1974; "This is the new revitalised, vitamin-drenched Purple that's been designed to erase memories of an ego-maimed five piece that finally erupted into many parts following a Japanese tour last June. Ian Gillan, the glamour-puss vocalist who is attributed with most of the blame for the wreckage, has not been gravely missed by fans after all, and, ever since his departure, has been behaving with mysterious unpredictability... The other Purple member who hasn't been sorely missed is bassist/producer Roger Glover. According to Lord, Glover became more and more weary and ill as the group's personality disorders reached new levels of absurdity — 'The main personality conflicts were between Ritchie and Ian,' says Lord, 'and that led to a general feeling of lethargy among everyone in the band. Towards the end we didn't even bother talking to each other. It got to the point where Ian was travelling to gigs in a separate car and was booking in at a separate hotel. I don't think it was really Ian's fault or Ritchie's fault. It's just one of those intangible things.' — Glover, it seems, was rarely more than a victim of the internal squabblings and, being "a very sensitive person," was markedly affected by the carryings on between Gillan and Blackmore. 'But I sometimes get the feeling he's kind of sorry he ever left,' says Lord. 'Everything is so much tighter these days'."

> **Had to buy "Stormbringer"**
> AFTER HEARING that Deep Purple's new album "Stormbringer" was in the shops, I had to buy it instantly, but there was one snag, no money, so I had to sell three of my old albums that I never played to get the money. — **Philip Mack, Thorpe Bay, Southend.**

It was reported of a show at Dundee's Caird Hall in *New Musical Express* in April 1974; "The firepower is stepped up several hundred watts for Purple's set. Either you fall to the ground in pain or join in the revivalist fervour and let the whole spectacle wash you clean. Kids explode into a besotted rage as soon as the lights fall on Blackmore, who hammers open the intro to 'Burn'. Half the crowd are doing a weird one-legged Purple stagger that takes them careering around the hall crashing into startled security men. Sabbath crazees (sic) specialise in the hunched-up double-barrelled victory salute whereas Purple freaks want nothing so crass. Their finishing touch is a wild, one-armed royal wave that can be performed as a companion to the Purple Stagger or from a seated position and embellished with a simple neanderthal grunt. Stranger still are the activities on stage, where each Purple member has his own tortured brand of patented self-expression. Most subtle and absorbing of all are the worm movements of Ritchie Blackmore, whose singed hair and black wet-look shirt and slacks give him just the right air of brooding chicness, except we've seen most of it before from Jimmy Page. Blackmore exhibits the same black arrogance offstage, making him the least likeable and the most interesting of the whole Purple crew. Dave Coverdale's technique is the illusion of sustained orgasm. His chief prop is a telescopic mic stand that he opens and closes at crotch level all the while pouting, jabbing out his chin and punching a fist in the air. Bassist Glenn Hughes' epileptic mannerisms fall somewhere between those of Coverdale and the stripped-off, trench-digging style of drummer Ian Paice. Jon Lord kneels, leans and poses by his keyboards — and is little more absorbing than a man at a workbench. Again the sound is fuzzed over, and Coverdale and Hughes' two-tone harmonies glop together and stew along in the general furore. There's still the feeling that Purple are out for easy crowd reaction via demonstrations of firebrand aggro, as against reaching for the kind of music that's well within their reach. Blackmore in particular is a fine and underrated player who, despite his excellence on the recorded versions of tracks like 'Burn' and 'Mistreated', goes loop-brained the minute he's faced with a crowd. And the kind of neatly-flexed dynamics present on most Zeppelin tracks are nowhere to be found in the bustle of 'Might Just Take Your Life' or 'You Fool No One'. But just tell any of that to the crowd, who are so sticky with delight even Patsy and Jim of Artist Services are milling around with more than their usual air of casual involvement. And that pair have been around for the worst nights of Led Zep and the Stones. It's an enormous reception, naturally. By the time the band's two-hour set is through, most of the kids are totally spent and flop together in a tight little wad against the front of the stage. 'It's getting bleedin' hot up here,' shouts Glenn. The crowd wheezes along in agreement. Jon Lord, shirt buttons popped open and dragging on a cigarette like some wolfish cardsharp, breaks up the set to introduce the two new boys: Glenn, who they stole from Trapeze after watching the band at the Marquee; and Dave, who was spirited away from a Redcar boutique and sounds as close to Paul Rodgers as dammit. 'Yarr. Yarr. Yarrr. Pupple. Pupple,' the crowd yell back. They go completely wanton for 'Smoke On The Water' and other hot tricks circa Gillan and Glover. The final section degenerates into some dogged solo playing that has no visible point of departure or re-entry and probably exists as Purple's answer to all those critics who say they don't know a semi-tone from a Buster Keaton movie. The encore is Don Nix's 'Going Down', and you can just spot the muscular frame of a bouncer pinned the wrong way round against the stage front. Earlier he'd walked his rippling biceps several times past Jim and Patsy, but this man has no brains to get caught in a situation of that sort."

It was reported in *Sounds* in April 1974; "Jon Lord strolled from the keyboards to the centre of the Odeon stage and told a jam packed wildly enthusiastic Edinburgh audience — 'Last time we were here was a long time ago. The next number is 'Donald Where's Yer Troosers', seriously folks, we've got something different for you this time. We stole Glenn Hughes from Trapeze. We're paying him £12.10 a week and he's worth every penny. We couldn't find a singer at first to replace Ian, then we found David Coverdale' — Deep Purple, as they were, would have effortlessly packed this place twice over. With two relatively new faces in the band, they arrived this time, after what had been an agonising eighteen months' delay for most of these customers, with something, shall we say in the way of intrigue. How would they sound with Hughes and Coverdale in the shoes of Glover and Gillan? Would things ever be the same? The answer must be an emphatic yes judging strictly on this performance. Purple's brand of rock hasn't crumbled away. Coverdale using 'Mistreated' from the *Burn* album as the best possible proving ground, came over loud (which should go without saying), clear and real powerful-like in a bluesy piece that took off with Ritchie Blackmore's guitar wailing compulsively. There were other obligatory items such as 'Smoke On The Water' which brought all eighteen hundred disciples to their feet. But the glowing embers from 'Burn' were what really mattered here. 'You Fool No One' was another, starting with Lord, like some abominable Dr Phibes, draped over the organ, giving us all a giggle with a patronising 'Scotland The Brave' and 'Flight Of The Bumble Bee' before getting down to business. When Blackmore took over in the number, turning it into a sort of one man show with a bluesy virtuoso display, this was Purple people eaters at their characteristic best. Fortunately they've lost nothing in the changes. They're still abundantly equipped to take good care of business."

With *Burn* and the *California Jam* to their name by mid 1974, whilst Mk3 still weren't immune from the comparisons to Mk2, they were in an excellent position overall. It was reported in the *Coventry Evening Telegraph* on 25th May 1974; "Deep Purple are on at the Coventry Theatre on Tuesday, but if you miss them then, they'll be there on Wednesday evening for an extra show. The Purple tour is their first since Roger Glover and Ian Gillan left the band and their biggest British tour since 1972. There were doubts about how the band would fare when Glover and Gillan split but the replacements, Dave Coverdale and Glenn Hughes, who played with Trapeze, have more than made up for the loss. The vocal power on Purple's latest album, *Burn*, is perhaps stronger than before, and Coverdale has shown writing ability by helping to compose most of the tracks on the album. *Burn* is already deservedly a big seller, and doubtless it will continue to rise as a result of the band's live appearances. Supporting them will be American band, Elf, whose debut album, *Carolina County Ball*, was produced by Roger Glover."

## Mk3 As A Live Band

*Sounds* reported in June 1974; "Purple hit Coventry with two evenings of good music and sheer lunacy to mark the end of a triumphant British tour. Everything seemed quite normal at the opening of Elf's set. They have developed into a highly polished professional unit. Ronnie Dio displayed his powerful vocals on a searing rendition of 'Happy' from their current album *Carolina County Ball* and the delivery of this number was so crisp and powerful that the audience surged towards the stage in appreciation. Suddenly from nowhere a 'dirty great big' bag of flour hit Ronnie on the head. More of them seemed to appear from the corners of the stage and soon enough the whole line-up of Stephen Edwards (guitar), Craig Gruber (bass), Mickey Lee Soule (piano) and Cool Guy (drums) were covered in dat (sic) white stuff. The audience, who were looking a bit dead, didn't seem to react to this attack. Next on were Purple, kicking the set off in fine form with 'Burn'. They played their asses off and the set ran smoothly apart from a mysterious incident involving a bottle breaking against the side of Glenn Hughes leg. Blackmore featured some really fine soloing and Ian Paice did a mindblasting solo in 'You Fool No One' which went into 'Mule'. David Coverdale displayed his vociferous vocals in 'Mistreated'. It was a great set, not their best, but they were out to have a good time. They too were bombarded with flour at the end of 'Space Truckin''. By this time the audience were on their feet and cheering and the band came back on for an encore which was 'Going Down' which culminated with a line of trouserless roadies having a knees up across the stage. To finish this off a certain gentleman, who has been described as the entertainments officer, strode across the stage in black tights, knee length boots and hat, looking like the son of Max Wall, and bared his buttocks to all. Backstage after the show the scene was comparatively calm. Jon, Dave and Glenn were getting ready for their trip to Germany the next day where they will be performing Jon's *Gemini Suite* and everyone was bidding each other farewell. Two burly characters confronted me 'don't forget to mention Pad of the plank and Jim for their excellent job on security' — uh okay, boys. This tour has proved the new line-up to be a viable proposition, and this is obviously a skeleton of what to expect in the months to come." (To correct the misinformation in the article, it was *Windows* that was due to be performed).

In October 1974, *Melody Maker* reviewed a performance that took place in September in Berne, Switzerland; "Despite their second billing to the local heavy heroes Deep Purple (whose *Machine Head* and *Burn* albums were recorded in Switzerland and have sold fantastically here), the sensational Alex Harvey Band came near to stealing an impressive show... Deep Purple are well entrenched in the hearts of Swiss fans. With a bellowed 'how are yer?' from Dave Coverdale, the band belted into 'Burn', featuring some expert mic stand twirling from the singer, a brief flash of Jon Lord and some fast Ritchie Blackmore guitar. Although the set which followed sent many fans into idiot dancing ecstasy, Purple provided few new ideas. The act followed the pattern used on Purple's recent British tour — 'Burn' gave way to 'Might Just Take Your Life' with some fine vocal duetting between Coverdale and bassist Glenn Hughes, and an extended Lord solo. Then came 'Lay Down, Stay Down' with Ritchie playing at a frantic pace and even tuning the guitar without losing noticeable speed. The best number of the evening for me was 'Mistreated' with some beautiful Blackmore playing, almost lyrical at times, and some nice bass counterpoint from Hughes. Dave Coverdale's lyrics reminded me of some of Eric Burdon's better live versions of 'Don't Let Me Be Misunderstood'."

A performance in Houston was reviewed in *Melody Maker* in September 1974; "The massive air conditioned confines of the Astrodome finally got its first taste of rock 'n' roll and although the introduction was unusually harsh the 'dome

## Mk3 As A Live Band

still stands. There was a security system to protect the precious Astroturf which seemed to entice rebellion among the young fans and they strained to the limit on J. Geils' encore and then completely overran it as Deep Purple appeared. It was almost a military battle until the classic human wave rock strategy prevailed and Deep Purple's thunderous crashings and dro8888ning electronics provided a suitable warfare soundtrack. Deep Purple did nothing unusual or subtle enough to diminish their reputation as one of the reigning decibel demons of the rock world. There were plenty of endless distorted guitar solos, a lot of sore throated vocalising and a large helping of the obligatory smoke bombs. Suffice to say that they played very loud for a long time and incited their fans to mindlessness, and occasionally reckless physical deeds... Guitarist Geils was his usual self, which put the audience at Deep Purple's doorstep although it probably wasn't necessary... It was the fifth rock concert of the summer that drew 25,000 fans in Houston and hopefully it has opened the unique indoor comfort of the Astrodome for less noisy and more peaceful

### Deep Purple

DEEP PURPLE'S recent concert at the huge Long Beach Arena was a bit of a letdown after their classic performance at the now historic Ontario Festival. The relatively new band (David Coverdale and Glenn Hughes just finishing their second album with them) performed a satisfying show length-wise (near two hours) but the music itself seemed to lack a vitality and enthusiasm which was so present during their earlier outdoor concert.

The show was festival-style seating (no chairs on the floor but with a balcony above) which does not make for the greatest of visual and aural conditions but the brilliance of guitarist Ritchie Blackmore and drummer Ian Paice more than compensated. Blackmore is a showman all the way but what is more important is his almost unequalled playing. His fingers seem to float over the maple necks on his Stratocasters like doves in flight but when the time comes for Ritchie to rock, he's ready. Ian is a perfect complement for Blackmore's guitarmanship, providing a gut-level rhythm interspersed with unbelievable fills.

Newcomers Hughes and Coverdale are weak links at best; bassist Glenn is adequate but his screechings on vocals are unbearable; vocalist David has neither a strong voice nor a memorable one and you can only envision Paul Rodgers in his place. Material included the title track from their newest album ("Stormbringer") as well as the standard arrary of oldies ("Space Truckin'", "Smoke On The Water," et al).

— STEVE ROSEN.

rock presentations. This night will be remembered as the one on which the 'dome fell beneath the onslaught of rock 'n' roll for the first time."

The Houston Astrodome was the world's first multipurpose domed sports stadium. Just as well really. Blackmore was quoted in *Circus Raves* in January 1975; "When you're out there in these mammoth outdoor gigs, it's impossible to play well. You've got a wind whipping around you, throwing you off all the time, and it's so cold you can't warm up. I don't mind the large halls half as much as these open-air things… I'd rather play a nice sizable auditorium for a few nights in a row than play to 50,000 people outside in the wind. There is no way to play well on an open-air gig. If it rains, it's really all over, but there are other things that happen as well. We've scheduled our next tour so that we don't play any more than three nights in a row, otherwise it's unfair on our fans."

When it came to touring after the release of *Stormbringer*, collectively, everyone in Deep Purple had mixed feelings about the album. David Coverdale was quoted of *Stormbringer* in *Disc* in November 1974; "I am really chuffed to death with it. I think it's a logical progression from *Burn*. We've explored the themes more now, and I'm very pleased with the way they've worked out. It was the first time I'd written anything since *Burn* was completed and it was done in rather a hurry. Theoretically we had a couple of weeks of peace and quiet to write in but inevitably they turned into a couple of weeks of revelry and we found most of the writing was actually done while we were in the studio."

In November 1974, *The San Francisco Examiner* reviewed a performance that took place at The Cow Palace; "Deep Purple, a vulgar and raunchy collection of noisemakers, headlined the bill. Following close behind, but musically at least occasionally interesting, was the septet known as the Electric Light Orchestra. Predictably, if the electronic noises are loud, the staging outrageous, the lyrics inaudible and the melody non-existent (all characteristics of Deep Purple) the audience will reflect a similar lack of taste and decency. Fireworks were thrown on stage, flaming torches illuminated portions of the Cow Palace from time to time, teenagers reeled through the aisles spaced-out or drunk and the combined stench of pot smoke and vomit flowed through the jam-packed arena. If the vaudeville stage act and racket that Deep Purple pass off as music are the end result of the musical migration that the Beatles and Stones started a decade ago then I'm in favour of pulling the plug on British musical immigration. Deep Purple sells lots of LPs and attracts huge crowds everywhere, a comment more on teenage taste than the group's musical integrity. Their performance starts with an electric blast of noise accompanied by screams from singer (?) David Coverdale and bassist Glenn Hughes. Dry-ice 'smoke' billows from the stage. 'Burn' is the first number, a searing jangle of shattering sounds. Next comes 'Might Just Take Your Life', somewhat better because the only Deep Purpler who has real class, guitarist Ritchie Blackmore (who composes most of their stuff) gets in some solo licks. Then it's 'Stormbringer', not only ungrammatical but also unmusical — more noise. 'Gypsy', short on shouting and Hughes is one of the most objectionable rock-shouters I've ever observed gets rather quickly into nice guitar and a suggestion that keyboard player Jon Lord probably knows his instruments if only he could be heard over the din. The set continued without improvement from 'Lady Double Dealer' to 'Mistreated' (both Blackmore's) and on, and on."

Not everyone liked the loudness of Deep Purple live. Blackmore has often argued that to get the most out of Deep Purple's music is to engage with the subtleties in it but in fairness, maybe it is hard to do that when the volume is up at eleven. The *Daily Press* reported in December 1974; "With the state the economy's in it was no wonder Norfolk Scope was only half full for an evening with Deep Purple, Electric Light Orchestra (ELO) and Elf. The Tuesday night concert was the last stop on the American tour and England's ELO and Purple warned the audience that the evening was going to be one of those 'anything goes' happenings with good music and good times for all. And, at least for ELO, it was... Deep Purple had a big job in trying to surpass their support act and though they tried their best they were hard pressed to match up. The group, led by guitarist, Richard Blackmore, played with enough energy and volume to cause half of Norfolk to blackout, and most of the audience to follow suit. Purple's first number was the title track from the *Burn* album, released earlier this year and, because of the volume, left ears flapping to the sonic breeze. With one's fingers in one's ears you were able to cut through the distortion and reverberation and accurately hear the music through the noise."

Upon being asked why he thought Deep Purple sold so many albums, Blackmore was quoted in *Sounds* in February 1975; "I don't know, I don't buy 'em. I have no idea, I can't be objective about listening to them and the LPs but not about how it sells or why or anything to do with that at all. On stage we have a lot of intense excitement, it's like a nervous, adrenalin kind of thing. People either love it or they get scared of it. That's why we maybe have a lot of people who hate us because we're so demanding. What we put down you can't talk over and we don't want anybody talking over it. So they either say nothing or they leave; that's why, for instance, we get no radio play in England because the housewives can't do their dusting when we're playing on the radio, it probably interferes with the Hoover or something."

Perhaps it was the case that the scale of excitement from *Burn* and from the California Jam was such that anything that Deep Purple did immediately after that was bound to be met with, at least some extent of, disappointment. On the one hand there's the argument of *"Burn* was great and so was *Stormbringer*, there was certainly more mileage in this line-up had Blackmore wanted to continue with it" but then on the other hand, it is plausible that post *Burn* and post California Jam, there may have been a sense of (for both Blackmore, the fans, and the media), "where does Deep Purple go from here? How can they top that?".

A performance was reviewed in *Sounds* in December 1974; "Deep Purple's recent concert at the huge Long Beach Arena was a bit of a letdown after their classic performance at the now historic Ontario festival. The relatively new band (David Coverdale and Glenn Hughes just finishing their second album with them) performed a satisfying show length wise (near two hours) but the music itself seemed to lack a vitality and enthusiasm which was so present during their earlier outdoor concert. The show was festival style seating (no chairs on the floor but with a balcony above) which does not make for the greatest of visual and aural conditions but the brilliance of guitarist Ritchie Blackmore and drummer Ian Paice more than compensated. Blackmore is a showman all the way but what is more important is his almost unequalled playing. His fingers seem to float over the maple necks of his Stratocasters like doves in flight but when the time comes for Ritchie to rock, he's ready. Ian is a perfect complement for Blackmore's guitarmanship, providing a gut level rhythm interspersed with unbelievable fills. Newcomers Hughes and Coverdale are weak links at best — bassist Glenn is adequate but his screechings on vocals are unbearable. Vocalist David has neither a strong voice nor a memorable one and you can only envisage Paul Rodgers in his place. Material included the title track from their newest album (*Stormbringer*) as well as the standard array of oldies ('Space Truckin'', 'Smoke On The Water' et al.)."

It's fascinating how the reviewer still described Hughes and Coverdale as the new guys considering that by this point, they had made a significant musical contribution to the Mk3 line-up as both writers and musicians. Perhaps the reviewer was missing the sound of Mk2 Deep Purple. Besides, relatively speaking, as prominent as Mk3 Deep Purple's was, it barely spanned for just over a year in the grand scheme of things. And Glenn Hughes vocals, well, they're quite marmite aren't they as in, some people really go for the high-pitched screaming harmonies but certainly, they're not everyone's cup of tea.

It was reported in *Melody Maker* in February 1975; "Cleveland Ohio, Jon Lord swayed back and forth at the organ, eyes closed, matching the intensity of Ritchie Blackmore's furious chording. Continuing to play, he opened his eyes and motioned frantically to a roadie nearby, 'Where are we?' he shouted over the roar of the music, 'Smoke On The Water', the roadie yelled back. Lord wasn't satisfied, 'No man, Where *are* we?!' 'Oh!' the roadie got the message, 'Cleveland!!' Jon Lord smiled. True story, but even if it was made up it'd be appropriate because Deep Purple recently completed their nineteenth tour of America, and that one adds up to one hell of a lot of cities. Their shows were predictable — in the good sense. You could rely on Ritchie to make you hair stand on end. You could rely on Paice's precision pounding to produce the gut reaction you need from rock and roll. And you could rely on the songs. But American audiences learned they could rely on one more thing — Deep Purple's continued artistic development with the transition of Glenn Hughes and David Coverdale from relative newcomers to major contributors to the group, and powerful, confident artists in their own right. With Lord now approaching thirty-four and Hughes and Coverdale both at twenty-three, Purple sports a combination of maturity and vitality that few bands can match. Hughes ensures a certain vocal versatility the group has never before enjoyed and provides another first for the band — a rhythmically interesting bass. And Coverdale, in fact, delivers a vocal performance in 'Mistreated' that's one of

## Mk3 As A Live Band

the true highlights of the show."

Luckily, a number of the very last live performances of Mk3 were recorded. Whilst there is no shortage of live recordings of Deep Purple, it is great that some of the most significant dates are available as live recordings because overall, they are demonstrative of the fact that even though Ritchie Blackmore was just days away from calling it a day with the band, everyone was still playing with professionalism and putting on a good show, both theatrically (judging by the audience reaction!) and musically. That is certainly noteworthy and testament to the fact that Deep Purple had a professional attitude towards the music and their audience as in, even if some members were unhappy to the point of wanting to leave the band at times (and I don't just mean Blackmore), there still seemed to be a professional perseverance that is apparent on such recordings.

The recordings exist because whilst the band weren't certain that Blackmore wanted to quit, management wanted to ensure that they had material available for release in the event of the band splitting up. By this point, rumours of Blackmore wanting to quit were in circulation and amongst some colleagues more than others. Coverdale was quoted in *New Musical Express* in August 1975; "We started the last European tour with Ritchie still a full member. After we'd done a couple of dates I began to feel strange vibes and knew something was going on. I went to see Rob Cooksey and I could just tell from his eyes that he was keeping something from me. I could sense that he didn't want to commit himself because Ritchie has told him something in private and he didn't want to break that confidence, even though it concerned us all business wise."

Rob Cooksey might have been more in the know what with having been witness to the musical rapport that Blackmore had with Dio when making the first Rainbow album. *Radio & Records* reported in March 1975; "Joe Smith presented Gold albums to Deep Purple for *Stormbringer*, their latest

LP. Joining Smith in his office are Purple members Ian Paice, David Coverdale, Glenn Hughes and Jon Lord. Not shown are Ritchie Blackmore and manager, Rob Cooksey, who were in Germany at the time of presentation."

On balance though, the rumours had been circulating for some time and even though the following report is from April 1975 (by which time Blackmore had left Deep Purple), it sheds a little bit of light onto some of the factors that may have been fuelling the rumours prior to his departure. *Sounds* reported in April 1975; "Ritchie Blackmore may split from Deep Purple. Rumours concerning this have been rife for some weeks now, so much so in fact that three weeks ago EMI issued a press release denying a possibility of a breakup. But *Sounds* believes that, following the completion of his solo album, *Rainbow* in Munich, Blackmore may amicably part from Purple and form a band with the musicians who backed him on his solo effort. The remaining Purple members will stay together. A spokesman from Purple's offices this week said, 'the band is splitting, but only for three or four months to enable Ritchie to promote his solo album'."

David Coverdale was quoted in *Rolling Stone* in November 1975; "I'd known something was up after Ritchie finished his solo album. Nothing definite, but Ritchie was always staying away from us socially." Glenn Hughes stated in his autobiography; "I can't remember how I found out that Ritchie was leaving. It would have been in January 1975, right after we played a festival at Sunbury in Melbourne, Australia. The management at the time was switching to a new manager called Rob Cooksey, who is a pretty tough guy and doesn't take shit from anybody. I think Ritchie wanted to be in control of his band and to make Bach-influenced classical rock music, which is why he formed Rainbow."

Blackmore was quoted in *Rolling Stone* in April 1975; "Nobody knows I'm up to this. I just want to prove a point to myself that I can do it on my own. I don't want to do a big solo thing. There will never be a Ritchie Blackmore Band. Everybody knows who's leading a group, you don't have to mention his name in the title. Besides, I couldn't handle the responsibility. For now this is my weekly toy, but who knows what'll happen if it takes off."

Mk3 Deep Purple's three final live shows were recorded; Graz in Austria on 3rd April, Saabrücken in Germany on 5th April and Paris on 7th April, 1975. The material recorded at Saabrücken features strongly on *Made In Europe*, released in 1976. Recordings of the Graz and Paris shows were released later on *Mk3: The Final Concerts*, in 1996. They are also available as individual releases.

All releases provide an insight into how Deep Purple were performing live at the time and what their setlist was like. They feature a good mix of Mk3 songs from both *Stormbringer* and *Burn*, the point being that even where not everyone was pleased with *Stormbringer*, the songs from the album were used comfortably and played tightly live. The set included 'Stormbringer', 'The Gypsy' and 'Lady Double Dealer' as well as from *Burn*, the title track, 'You Fool No One' and 'Mistreated'. Staple Deep Purple material is also included; 'Smoke On The Water' and 'Space Truckin''.

Ultimately, considering that Deep Purple had a strong choice of songs for their setlist by this time and considering that for many fans and band members, *Stormbringer* divided opinion, the material from the album was considered worthy for live shows and rightly so. Although the musical differences on *Stormbringer* were ultimately accountable for Blackmore leaving the band, the album and its content is certainly not without merit in and of itself. And what's more is that Deep Purple played them well live. Graz is well worth a listen because it goes some way towards contesting the narrative that *Stormbringer* was something to be displeased with.

By the time Deep Purple had begun touring in Europe in 1975, with Blackmore having recorded his first Rainbow album, considering that Blackmore's priorities were elsewhere, his live performances certainly didn't give the game away. I'm not certain where this quote is from (that's newspaper clippings for you!) but Jon Lord was quoted of the situation; "Ritchie is a pro from top to bottom. He carried on playing even though he wasn't happy with the situation."

Graz, even prior to being released officially, the recording was considered to be an excellent capture of Mk3 playing live. 'Burn' on the officially released Graz album is played with high energy — from the riff, through to the vocals. Deep Purple Mk3 certainly doesn't sound like a band on its last legs. The solo sections are long and engaging. Also, the Mk2 material is given a fantastic Mk3 treatment in the form of Glenn Hughes' vocal harmonising on the second verse of 'Smoke On The Water'. And of course, the call and response rapport between Blackmore and Lord is ever present on a twenty-minute rendition of 'Space Truckin''.

Mk3's final show recorded in Paris on 7th April 1975 was Ritchie Blackmore's last one with Deep Purple until Mk2 reformed for the *Perfect Strangers* tour and album in 1984 (Blackmore left Deep Purple forever during the 1993 tour, *The Battle Rages On*). Paris in 1975 contains every song that is present on the Graz 1975 album with the addition of both 'Going Down' and 'Highway Star' (this is possibly why some fans consider it to be the case that the Graz album is not a full recording of the show there).

It would be so easy to expect the Paris 1975 recording to be worthy listening from a historic perspective more than a musical one but this simply isn't the case; yes, Paris 1975 is fascinating because it is Mk3's last ever performance together but equally, despite the fact that Blackmore already had his eyes on the exit by then, the music doesn't seem to have suffered for it.

Listen to Paris 1975 and compare it to Deep Purple's performance at the California Jam in April 1974 and there doesn't seem to be a marked absence of energy, enthusiasm and of course, skill. In particular, Paris 1975 exhibits an excellent rendition of 'Stormbringer', showing once again that although not everyone in the band liked the track, they were willing and able to do it justice onstage. Equally, 'The Gypsy' (a track that Blackmore was probably more keen on due to it being more guitar oriented) is played with emotion; melancholy and careful thought.

Of course, by this point in his career, it is highly plausible that Blackmore wouldn't have had difficulty playing very well, even if he wanted to be elsewhere at the time. But either way, is the recording of Paris 1975 reflective of a band giving it their all? Well, it certainly sounds to be the case. The same applies in his fast and furious playing of the 'Lady Double Dealer' riff; it is done with speed, accuracy and style. The rest of the set is as much of a joy to listen to as Graz 1975. It offers the same level of excellence whilst being musically different enough in the solos to be worthy of attention in comparison to the similar sets recorded just days earlier.

As before, Coverdale and Hughes do justice to the Mk2 material with 'Smoke On The Water' and 'Space Truckin''. Throughout Mk3's tenure, it's fascinating to observe how Coverdale and Hughes worked with the two songs in terms of what they added to them live and how they made them their own. For instance, it is noticeable how they developed their ideas with the Mk2 material when comparing Paris 1975 to the album, *Live In London* (recorded on 22nd May 1974). It's fair to say that Coverdale and Hughes certainly didn't replicate what Ian Gillan did with the material but on balance, they probably weren't trying to either. Even lyrically there are strong examples of this. In 'Smoke On The Water', Gillan sang "*we* all went down to Montreux" but on account of the

## Deep Purple - Stormbringer: In-depth

fact that Coverdale wasn't part of the history that informed the song, he sang it as *"they* all went...". Essentially, Deep Purple Mk3's last live show is easily demonstrative of a band that had more mileage, had they all wanted to continue with it and had musical differences not been what they were on *Stormbringer.*

And to think that on the surface of things, the Mk3 tour of Europe in 1975 didn't start off too badly. It was reported in *Sounds* in March 1975; "As far as Britain's concerned everything has seemed quiet on the Purple front recently. We got a taste of their brand of hard rock last year in a tour where they introduced their two new cohorts, Hughes and Coverdale. Two albums later the band have re-established themselves comfortably and still maintain their position as big cookies in the rock 'n' roll league table. The fact that the band were the first big, big biggies to play Yugoslavia makes a story in itself. When an Eastern European government offers to pay a whole hunk of Dinars (the local coinage y'know) for a rock band to play their local baseball halls you know this means a good story. So what's the story? After a three month lay off, the Purple family reunite to take on Europe, their strongest territory. To open the tour they kick off in the land of the red star. This was a totally new experience to both the band and Yugoslavia, and like two virgins the enterprise was entered with eager application but a certain amount of caution."

In the same issue of *Sounds,* it was reported of Deep Purple's performance in Belgrade, Yugoslavia that took place on 16th March; "The band did their sound check in the hall — the first time they played together since an Australian festival (Sunbury) three months previously. The first few minutes were spent balancing the sound, the hall bare and echoey (sic). The first two numbers 'Stormbringer' and 'Lady Double Dealer' sounded loose but the ol' Purple magic began to creep in on a thunderous rendition of 'Mistreated'. Coverdale's vocals pierced the hall's emptiness with razor like sharpness. By the time the band were ready to make their entrance on stage that night, the audience were in an epileptic frenzy. The hall was as full as it could be, the police looking sinister in their khaki uniforms, red stars on their caps. As Blackmore belted out the opening chords of 'Burn', dry ice smoke filled out the front half of the hall and the momentum and excitement built up to a terrifying peak. Musically the concert was a zillion times better than it could have been, due to the audience response. Purple feed off their audience reaction and vice versa. This is what makes them the most exciting band in the world, and the fact they have five of the most talented musicians around. The best two numbers of that night were 'Mistreated' and 'You Fool No One' but the set began to meander on 'Space Truckin''. The band returned with the final punch on the encore 'Going Down', featuring a forceful slide solo from Blackmore, who emptied the contents of his slide (a bottle full of brandy) onto the surprised press enclosure. David Coverdale's and Hughes' vocals and interchanges were excellent — a good opening night. The audience went bananas."

The same issue also reported on the performance in Zagreb, the following day; "Zagreb is a different kettle of goulash altogether, the hotel was very accommodating and the attendants seemed unperturbed by the band's arrival. The audience at the hall made the Belgrade mob look timid. Crackers were exploding everywhere and the bouncers looked less menacing. The atmosphere in the hall was overwhelming, the same excitement that must have been buzzing around when The Beatles were at their peak. This was the event of events and the kids were going to make the most of it. The band kicked off with 'Burn', the epitome of opening numbers, crashing chords and thunderous screams amidst the swirling smoke. The crowd went ape whatsit again. Blackmore was calm for the most part of the concert, feeling his way around, building to a terrifying peak at one point during 'You Fool No One'. He's a guitarist who wavers from good to ultra brilliant, a versatile player, an underrated guitarist. At one point a girl tried to hand over a note to Blackmore. Before she had the opportunity to do so, a security guy punched her in the face. Blackmore returned the compliment by delivering a boot to the back of the squarehead heavy's head. 'He was about to pull out a gun on me,' Blackmore commented later, 'if he had tried anything, that guitar would have gone through his head' — At that point, Blackmore was at one of his more frantic points of the solo. The incident captured the intensity of his playing and showmanship. While Patsy and Jim (the Purple security men) tried to control the audience's enthusiasm without violence, the guards down below began taking their revenge on the kids but eventually gave up looking pale-faced and, hands over their ears, retired to the side of the stage. Ian Paice provided a tremendous solo during 'You Fool No One', which led into 'The Mule' while Lord seemed to be having trouble with his synths during 'Space Truckin''. The set finished as the audience just stood there, obviously not familiar with the good ol' British encore. The band returned to perform 'Going Down' and 'Highway Star'. The sound was a bit rough, the set loose in places but that Purple power was there bubbling away. 'I've got to admit I looked at those two sets as warm up gigs,' Blackmore said later, 'I know it's the wrong attitude but I was feeling my way round and the kids enjoyed themselves anyway'."

With fans going wild for them and Purple branching out to more diplomatically demanding locations of the day, had Deep Purple Mk3 wanted to carry on for a little bit longer, they could have done so. The audience demand was certainly there. In *Sounds* in March 1975, it was surmised of Deep Purple's two gigs in Yugoslavia; "The excitement of the whole affair almost made the gigs themselves superfluous. Admittedly they weren't Purple's finest hours but even at their worst they're bloody good. It wasn't exactly the welding of East/West relationships but it did indicate that music has a worldwide appeal, and if music is the language of the world, then Purple are multilingual."

Essentially, even when a little below par, audiences were keen to welcome them. But critically though, that's not what Blackmore wanted; he didn't want to lazily ride the crest of a wave that musically, he no longer felt inspired by. Soon after his departure he was quoted in *Modern Guitars* in 1975; "I'm just playing the music I want to play, the music I believe in. Whereas, with Purple, towards the end, I wasn't believing in the music. And as soon as you start disbelieving, really, people are gonna stop coming to see it. And I wasn't going to just sit through because it was another day, another dollar. This decision could lead me to be out of pocket. I mean, I was making a lot of money with Purple. Money is useless for giving value once you've reached a certain stage of music. You've just gotta take that chance. Say, 'well, it's a chance and I've been without money before. I'll live without it again. I'm playing music I want' or sit back and wine and dine and have a good time. I'm having a good time in this. I'm playing the music I want to play. I don't get off particularly on all the side effects that go with being successful. That's why I live quite simply. There are certain extravagances I like, which I won't mention because they're rude. There are some things I spend a lot of money on. But obviously I don't make much ado about money, and if it came to music or money — I'd take the music."

Blackmore was quoted in *The Los Angeles Times* in November 1975; "When I started to work with Ronnie. I had no intention of leaving Purple. At first we had just intended to do a single, but it went so well we decided to do a whole album. That's how our first album, *Ritchie Blackmore's Rainbow*, came about. I had to leave Purple because this new experience was so much more rewarding, especially working with a vocalist like Ronnie." After making the first Rainbow album, the plan was initially for Blackmore to go back to working with Deep Purple but in time, he found that it just didn't feel right. As he was quoted in *Modern Guitars* in 1975; "But then I thought, well, this is silly because there is such a difference between when I was back with Purple than when I'm working with this lot."

Really, it was pretty much the case that on the first night of the new Mk3 tour, Blackmore had really had enough. Like a kid who has just started the school term in September and is grieving that a fantastic summer break is over, Blackmore was probably thinking back to what a great time he had recording with Rainbow. He was quoted in *Modern Guitars* in 1975; "I had about six weeks off from Deep Purple before we started touring so I said, 'let's get together now.' We rushed about and rehearsed in two weeks, and we put the LP (*Ritchie Blackmore's Rainbow*) down in a month. And it all came together and it's come out. I'm being modest in saying it's kind of brilliant. It came out very well. After I did the LP and during making the LP, I was thinking about Purple and thinking it was so refreshing to be able to work with new musicians and to have a rapport that I didn't have with Deep Purple. It was just professionalism with Deep Purple rather than a rapport. Our drummer would be good enough to back anything, but not really to put any of his ideas forward, to make a song. It was, 'Whatever's there I'm gonna play and play very well.' With this particular setup (Rainbow), everybody listened to everybody else and would listen to ideas, whereas, Purple — myself included — got very blasé about other people's ideas. It was a case of, 'Well, let's just shove down, you know, more or less anything.' And it's a bit about money to a degree. It was getting to that stage where I was dreading to go into the studio. We finished the LP (*Ritchie Blackmore's Rainbow*) and I was really crazy about it. Then we had a tour with Deep Purple and after that first gig I realised I had been spoiled. During making this LP, I enjoyed it so much that now Deep Purple was becoming a hardship because everybody was egotistical, including myself. So, about halfway through the tour, I knew that we hardly spoke to each other. Not because everybody hated each other, but just because we had known each other so bloody long. It was really getting very hard to put together an LP. Nobody really had that many ideas. And what ideas were going around, I didn't particularly like. Most of the band was going towards funk and shoeshine music and I wanted to get back to rock. I had been very into classical the last few years, medieval music, very light music really… So, anyway, I got about halfway through the tour and I decided to tell the band (Deep Purple), I said, 'Look, I don't want to go into the studio' and they took it well."

Some of Mk3's live performances were such that it adds weight to the argument of "damn! Why didn't they keep going?!" but equally, there were certainly off days too. Whether this was down to reviewer opinion, tensions within the band or simply a bad day for some other random and unknown reason, it is worth being realistic about the fact that even at this stage in the band's tenure, they still divided opinion, and quite strongly at times too.

A live show was reviewed in *Acton Gazette* in May 1974 under the headline, "A Tidal Wave Of Noise Sweeps Over The Odeon"; "Deep Purple blasted the Hammersmith Odeon on Thursday with what must have been the loudest show ever at this particular venue. They were louder than loud, and it will be a long time before such a tidal wave of noise invades the Odeon again. You half expected the walls to crack up as organist Jon Lord and guitarist Ritchie Blackmore practically attacked their instruments. They were like two machine gunners. And their new singer, David Coverdale, seemed intent on singing even louder than the others were playing. You don't hear him sing, you feel it. And when he screams it's like being caught in the middle of an avalanche. But don't be misled into thinking that Purple gave a fabulous, exciting show. Because they didn't. The scene was set for a riot. The show was a sell out and the fans standing at the back had moved halfway down the aisles before it even started. Some of them boasted to the stewards that they were going to get up on stage. Before the start, the talk was of Ritchie Blackmore smashing up his guitar, and the kids could hardly wait. As it happened, they waited in vain. Some of them took their football scarves along, and they chanted 'We want Purple, we want Purple' — The Odeon should have been renamed the Hammersmith Kop for the night. The management had brought in special security men — ten massive sized bouncers with biceps like dumbbells, and wearing white t-shirts — to cope with any trouble. 'We won't have any problems here,' said one of them, 'they're just a load of kids, this is easy' — he was right. The lights went out, smoke drifted across the stage, Deep Purple had arrived. The audience roared and those standing surged down the aisles. They didn't get very far. The boys in white t-shirts sent them back nearly as fast as they had come down. A couple managed to break through, but they were quickly dispatched outside by the security men. The audience were well behaved after that. After such an opening, Purple were disappointing. It was strange, because the group is packed full of talent — Jon Lord, Ritchie Blackmore and Ian Paice are some of the highest rated musicians in the country. Sometimes Purple were very good, but too often the solos went on too long and didn't seem to be getting anywhere. Sometimes they were even boring and when Jon Lord played the theme from *2001*, it was embarrassing." It's worth noting that, whilst I've not transcribed them as such for ease of reading, the journalist spelt names as "John Lord" and "Richie Blackmore"; quite possibly he wasn't a Deep Purple fan.

    The *Stormbringer* album resulted in a significant change to the live sets whereby 'Stormbringer', 'The Gypsy' and 'Lady Double Dealer' replaced 'Lay Down, Stay Down' and 'Might Just Take Your Life'. All three songs from *Stormbringer* that were included in the live sets were ones that Blackmore had writing credits on. Clearly he still had influence on what would be played in the live sets compared to his control in the studio by that point.

Tellingly perhaps, at the end of Mk3's final performance in Paris, Coverdale thanked the crowd by saying "we hope to see you again in some shape or form."

> **Purple miss New York**
> DEEP PURPLE are on the States road right now and finish up on December 18 in Baltimore. The Purple lads are giving New York a miss this time round.

UK original album sleeve

UK test pressing

US original album sleeve

US test pressing

The EMI and Warner Bros releases differed not just in colourisation but also in the style of lettering. Both the UK and the US released test pressings. These "white labels" are released in very small quantities ahead of the release date so that the album can be checked for any potential imperfections in sound quality.

First press   Second press

The first 50,000 copies of the Japanese release included a poster. This was indicated on the obi strip. The second batch pressing had a changed obi strip. Collector's pay a premium for original Japanese pressings that still include the obi strip — a paper wrap around that includes information about the album. Having the obi strip still intact can invariably increase the value of the record significantly.

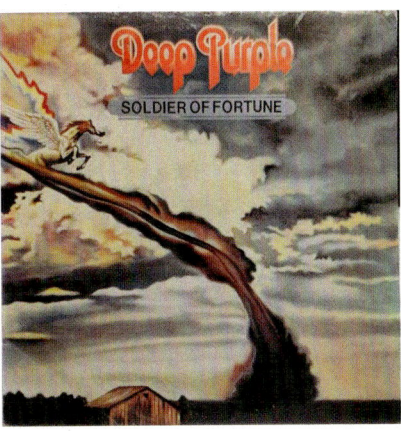

There were some unusual variations of the album sleeve around the world.
Top left: In Argentina the album's title is in Spanish.
Top right: In Korea the Ministry of Culture objected to the title track so it was omitted from the album which was renamed Soldier Of Fortune!
Bottom left and right: Unique Mozambique pressing with some inaccuracies with song titles on the back cover.

There was a quad mix of the album released by Warner Bros. The most noticeable difference was 'Soldier Of Fortune' which includes a different vocal take, where Coverdale sings a couple of lines with different phrasing.
This was released on both vinyl and on the now much rarer, open reel format.

*Greece*

*Uruguay*

*Columbia*

*Turkey*

For the majority of Europe Purple's albums were released on their own Purple label, formed in 1971. For some reason, Greece continued to release the albums on Harvest.
Whilst the album was licensed to Warner Bros for North America and Japan, other deals were done around the world. In Uruguay and Columbia it was released on Odeon and in Turkey on Stateside.

*France*

*Italy*

A couple of cassette variations that showed how the track order was changed for the format to balance the timings of both sides.

Yugoslavia

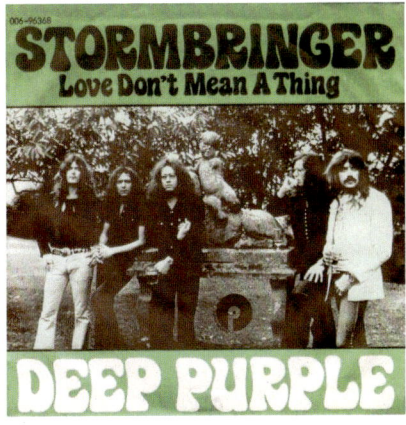
Denmark

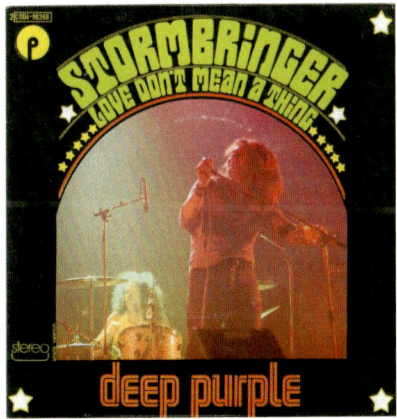
France

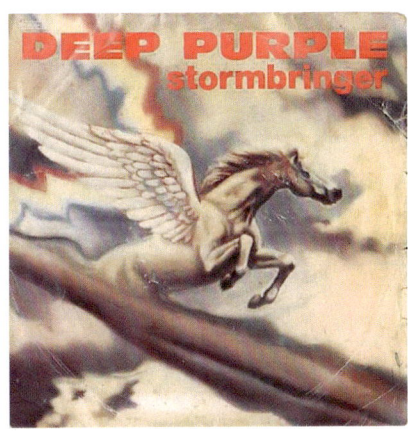
Italy

The album's title track was released as a single around the world with a unique selection of picture sleeves in most European countries.

Lady Double Dealer b/w You Can't Do It Right (With The One You Love) was a unique coupling to Japan. Warner Bros in North America used the Japanese B-side as the A-side and coupled it with High Ball Shooter. Venezuela also had its own unique coupling of Soldier Of Fortune b/w Stormbringer.

*USA*

*Venezuela*

# Chapter Five

## The End Of An Era?

Upon being asked to offer an overview of the personalities in Deep Purple Mk3, Jon Lord was quoted in *Melody Maker* in February 1975; "Okay, I'll start with Ritchie. He's difficult. I know him very well and he knows me very well. We have the ability to talk openly to each other, about pretty much anything, but I can't say that I'm his close friend. Except sometimes we find that, on the road, we're sitting in a bar somewhere by pure accident and we'll spend five hours together having a fabulous time. That's the anomaly of my relationship with Ritchie. And indeed Ritchie's relationship with most people. But they often find themselves suddenly surprised and walking out slightly dazed and thinking 'Christ, he's really such a nice guy when you get to know him' but then the next day he's probably going to totally ignore you. He's an introvert whose only extroversion is onstage. Ian Paice is a beaut. A great guy in my book. Not afraid of speaking his mind at all. With anybody. Least of all, members of the band. He's our kind of rock. He's always the steadying influence. Not an emotional man. I'm not saying that he's not capable of emotion but he doesn't use emotion to make judgements. He's the accountant of the band. If we want to know how much we earned on this tour, we have to ask Ian. David is still slightly bewildered by it all, though coping admirably and getting less bewildered every day. On the one hand he has this bewilderment and slight timidity about what's going on and on the other hand, it's really weird, his first tour as a professional was in the Starship. That's a helluva jump. Glenn I love. I absolutely adore that guy. He's a beautiful man. A little untogether — except onstage where he's very together. He's one of the most concerned musicians I've ever played with in terms of being concerned that the audience gets off, and it's not for Glenn's sake. To play with, he's an absolute dynamo and I meant to say that about Ian Paice too. There are times when I'm feeling a bit down, not really wanting to play and five bars into the first number I can't help it because Paicey's like a hand in your back, pushing you forward. He's a great musician's drummer. My main weakness is that I'm not really able to come up with the initial ideas for songs. My forte lies in developing the initial ideas. I find it very difficult to write a convincing riff, for instance, because I don't play guitar and the kind of rock and roll we play is very much a guitar oriented entity."

It was reported in *New Musical Express* in August 1975; "When *Rolling Stone* quoted Blackmore as saying he considered *Stormbringer* a 'load of shit' it seemed the end was nigh. 'Ritchie never said that,' insists Blackmore's mouthpiece, Cooksey, 'it was a terrible piece of misquoting. The writer didn't even put his name on the piece. Ritchie was really upset about it, especially because of what the other guys in the band must have thought'."

Rumours and gossip aside, Blackmore gave a comprehensive reason as to why he wasn't happy with *Stormbringer* when he was quoted in *The Los Angeles Times* in November 1975; "I had been bored with Purple for a long time. The band was getting complacent. In my opinion, nobody had their hearts in the music. Except for a few cuts, the last album sounded like the work of an average rock 'n' roll band. I didn't like the pressure of touring the world and then getting ten days off and having to go into the studio. What you get is an album that has two good songs and the rest padding. We were forcing the music, but we had to meet our album commitments. I've made plenty of money so I didn't want to go on in a situation I disliked. I wanted to get out before I got too bitter."

A lot of the time, it seems that discussion surrounding the musical differences present during the making of *Stormbringer* are often attributed to the funk and soul elements on the album that were brought in by Coverdale and Hughes. That's perhaps a bit of an unfair assessment to make on the basis that by this time, everyone was perhaps a bit fed up of each others' musical tastes and influences. Blackmore was quoted in *Record World* in June 1976; "There were too many directions in the band, all of us became too egotistical, including myself. It became like a five-way battle on stage. Which is good sometimes, but there wasn't too much unity in the band. There were no rehearsals and the writing was getting very scrappy... I like rock and medieval music, one extreme to the other. Ian Paice is into funk and jazz. Jon was just into classical. It is just that there were too many diverse things happening."

Blackmore was quoted in *Disc* in August 1975; "(Purple) seem to be pulling in diverse musical directions, and relying on a few musical clichés to tie it together... I'd stopped enjoying music with Purple. You must progress and I chose this (Rainbow) as my way of doing that."

Glenn Hughes was quoted in Martin Popoff's 2015 book, *Sail Away*; "With *Stormbringer*, we toured about a year and we were really at our height. Blackmore at the time was thinking of leaving, and I think from the genre of the songs that David and I were writing, like 'Hold On', 'You Can't Do It Right (With The One You Love)' and 'Holy Man', it was a little more apparent that it was becoming a crossover group. Ritchie always built his songs around the Bach guitar playing, and I really respected Ritchie for that because he was an originator, the first true innovator of that kind of music. I think he had gone as far as he wanted to go in Deep Purple. You know, I think the format of Gillan and Glover and all that stuff was a great metal band, whatever you want to call it... Look, you know, people have always said when Glenn Hughes and David Coverdale came into Deep Purple, it was like we changed the sound of the band from being a straight hard rock metal group to being a more bluesier, soulful, intelligent sounding music, I thought. When you replace guys like Gillan and Glover, you've got a come up — I don't sound like Roger Glover, of course, Roger doesn't sing. And I certainly don't sound like Ian Gillan, and neither does David. I think it was a really bold move to replace those two and have a top five record all around the world with *Burn*. The *Burn* record stands up for itself, it's brilliant. But Ritchie, midway through the *Stormbringer* tour, realised that the end was nigh for him, because the power was being taken from him, in the music. Because it was being written by all of us guys."

Coverdale was quoted in *New Musical Express* in August 1975; "Ritchie was worried about the direction he thought the band might be headed in. He didn't like the soul that was creeping into the band. See, what Ritchie regards as funk are things like 'Sail Away' and 'Mistreated' and that's the direction that the rest of the band saw us headed in... He was worried that the next album would be more bass oriented. He wanted to go out and get the things he really wanted to do, the guitar things, out of his system so that he could get into being a fifth of Deep Purple without feeling compromised. So he went out and decided to do his solo album. A lot of the songs on his album (*Ritchie Blackmore's Rainbow*) were ones that we rejected for *Stormbringer*. He put forward a lot of ideas he knew we wouldn't be interested in."

As was considered in *New Musical Express* in August 1975; "'Hold On' and the haunting, acoustic 'Soldier Of Fortune' on *Stormbringer* all marked changes for Purple — changes that the strong willed Blackmore found hard to tolerate. It was undoubtedly the introduction of bassist Glenn Hughes and Coverdale himself in 1973 that caused the marked realignment in Purple's approach. First came *Burn* which saw a hint of the band's infamous zomboid (sic) inhumanity being eaten away in favour of a more earthy approach. The pattern was exaggerated by months on the road to prove the worth of the new look outfit. As confidences grew, Blackmore's stranglehold over the band began to weaken. Then came *Stormbringer*, a surprise to many die hard Purple haters. It served as a consummation of the redirection its predecessor had pioneered. In essence, Blackmore's guitar no longer held the rest of the band at gun point. Glenn Hughes' bass had created a far stronger rhythm section with Jon Lord's organ and Ian Paice's drums. Not only stronger musically, but stronger mentally. The Blackmore regime was over... It's hard to imagine Blackmore, ego and all, wanting to return to Purple if his solo venture worked. Once he saw new influences come into the band that he didn't like and saw himself outvoted by the others, there was no way he could stay."

A particularly fascinating opinion that many people seem to subscribe to is the idea that *Stormbringer* signified the end of Deep Purple in the seventies. Of course, there was *Come Taste The Band* which followed *Stormbringer* in 1975 but with Blackmore's departure from Deep Purple, some people consider(ed) that this signified the end of Deep Purple. After *Stormbringer*, even Deep Purple weren't sure if they were still Deep Purple, at least by name.

When Blackmore left Deep Purple, David Coverdale started the search for a new band. He was quoted in *New Musical Express* in August 1975; "I suddenly realised I was calling Jon to play organ, Ian to play drums and Glenn to play bass, so I thought, 'what's the point of doing it solo, why not keep the band together?' We still own the name Deep Purple, as far as people and musicians. We decided to keep it going because we wanted to keep working together, nothing else. We can keep it going without Ritchie. I think Glenn and I proved the band could keep going and maintain its validity with new members."

Even in the early days of Mk3 Deep Purple, the band didn't strike a chord with everyone. *Burn* was reviewed in *New Musical Express* in February 1974; "New line-up time, folks. As you well informed young people will have been aware for nigh on a full season, Ian Gillan has left to be replaced by David Coverdale and Glenn Hughes from Trapeze is now in Roger Glover's chair. This album is the first to be produced under the new regime and, apart from the minimal amount of variation achieved by the use of two voices in various combinations instead of one, the amount of progress achieved has been negligible. What's always annoyed me about Deep Purple is that, while the first minute or so of most of their pieces is genuinely exciting, nothing ever happens afterwards, except that they drag it out for another five or six minutes while padding it out with numerous frenzied solos. There's the occasional unison tricky bit, and every so often Jon Lord does his Saturday-night-at-King's College routine, or Blackmore does a quick Hendrix pastiche, but basically it's the sound of Percy the singing pneumatic drill. The only variation is 'A 200', a piece of pointless pissing about for synthesiser and heavy rhythm section that could conceivably be entered as a replacement for the old *Doctor Who* theme. While vast numbers of people apparently find Deep Purple a wonderfully exciting group of young musicians, it only remains to point out that their current heavy sludge formula allows them almost no room whatsoever to demonstrate the undoubtedly high technical standards of musicianship that exist within the band. Without suggesting that they vault off into the Negative Zone in search of Yes vapour trail, a more adventurous musical policy may prove worthwhile. In other words, this is a loud, monotonous, rather messy and sadly uninspired album that only the hardest of the hardcore Purple freaks will have any use for at all."

It comes across that the reviewer's main complaint with *Burn* was that it wasn't progressive rock. But it wasn't really trying to be. It's like moaning that your dog is crap at being a cat. Perhaps. Whilst the reviewer was keen to assert that they didn't wish for Deep Purple to make an album that sounded like Yes, it comes across that they were bored of Deep Purple and perhaps considered them to be too formulaic for their tastes. That said, there were instances in which even members of Deep Purple complained that their sound had become too formulaic and they felt restricted in having to live up to expectations. By the time *Stormbringer* was released, there was perhaps a feeling that no matter what Deep Purple did, it would be met with criticism; if they stuck to hard rock and riff-oriented songs, they could have been met with criticism for not doing anything new and if they branched out into a different musical style then that could have been criticised for being too far off the mark in terms of the fan's expectations.

David Coverdale was quoted in *New Musical Express* in November 1974; "Purple is the sort of band that's got to the top and if there's any hint of them going down they'd call it a day. It's never been discussed with the band, but I certainly don't think they'd go down. I don't think they'd watch that happening. They'd rather retire up there, separate and go their individual ways, but leave the name of Deep Purple respected by the fans as it is. Each member of the band is very proud, particularly the trio that Glenn (Hughes) and I joined last year. And I'm quite sure they wouldn't ride downhill. What I mean is, if they felt they couldn't go any further — as they did with the last Deep Purple and the first Deep Purple — they'd change the band. But if they ever got that feeling with Glenn and I, I don't think they'd bother again. Glenn and I walked in with our bread buttered. It could have fallen on its ass, but fortunately it didn't, which I'm very proud of because it was a big pair of shoes I was standing in."

Where people subscribe to the idea that a Deep Purple album only really counts as such in instances where Blackmore is on guitar, *Stormbringer* could certainly mark the end of an era. Well, in 1975, it is plausible that this was a common feeling among fans. After all, if you consider that Mk2 was the point at which a lot of people really started to engage with Deep Purple's music, really, it was a big deal that Blackmore left Deep Purple in 1975, what with him having been not only a founding member, but a key innovator when it came to establishing the sound that would take the band onto large scale commercial success that ultimately began with *Deep Purple In Rock* in 1970. That is to say that if post *Stormbringer*, it was Ian Paice or Jon Lord who left Deep Purple, a similar extent of fan disappointment may have followed on the basis that Lord and Paice were also instrumental to Deep Purple as founding members of the band.

All musicians were incredibly important and whilst I don't wish to even attempt to elevate the status of anyone above the other, the fact is that with any lead guitarist being in the spotlight so much, it was perhaps inevitable that Blackmore's departure from Deep Purple was going to be felt to an extent that some fans may have been thinking that the remaining band would have been best off going by a different name entirely.

Maybe earning all the money that they were by the time of *Stormbringer* wasn't all that it was cracked up to be. Deep Purple were advised by their accountant that moving abroad would be the best way to avoid paying the high tax rates of home in the UK. Blackmore was the first of the band to move to America. In hindsight Jon Lord considered that, as much as he liked America, having to move there to California played a part in the downfall of his first marriage. The move to America was also awkward from an administration perspective because it meant that Deep Purple's communications with their London-based management became less accessible.

When it came to travelling, each band member had their own separate routines, unsurprising really considering that socially, they didn't spend a lot of time together. Ritchie Blackmore was quoted in Warner Bros.' November 1974 *Circular*; "I have two houses at the moment, one in England and one here in Oxnard. I'll probably move here within the next six months. Jon Lord and Ian Paice are coming out, Glenn Hughes may come as well. Dave Coverdale wants to go to Ireland. (The) tax situation is getting pretty bad over there." When asked if the circumstances he described would make it difficult to keep Deep Purple together, Blackmore was quoted, "Not really, we never socialise. We only meet when we're making an LP or when we're touring. We never — how do they say it? — hang out."

In *Sounds* in August 1975, Blackmore was quoted regarding the risk and uncertainty of leaving Deep Purple to start a new band; "Uncertain? Yes, I suppose it is. And for that reason, it's not boring. I feel so much easier now than I ever did with Purple. Take making records for example. Rainbow have a record deal where we make one album a year, and that's all I want to do. I made sure that was on the contract. Purple have a three albums a year deal, plus tours of the world. Consequently, when I was with them, the music was suffering and we were just turning out any old stuff. There was a lot of padding involved, which I think is exploiting the public to some extent. Also, I think it's better for a band on a long-term basis if the record company says, all right, one album a year, two at the most."

He was quoted in *Disc* in August 1975; "Whatever happens I think I've taken a valid chance which I had to try. What's more I respect all the material on the album, whereas there was a lot of padding on Purple albums, especially the latter ones."

Considering the overall frustrations that Blackmore was

faced with during the making of *Stormbringer*, his decision to leave Deep Purple is worthy of respect. For any artist, what would be the benefit of enduring something that felt creatively stifling? Ian Paice was quoted in Martin Popoff's 2015 book, *Sail Away*; "It wasn't so much David, it was the influence of Glenn. David was the new kid on the block and he was very malleable. He was just enjoying the vibe of being in a big rock 'n' roll band. Glenn's influences were so different, although on the first album, *Burn*, they were kept under control. When it came down to getting down to the second one, *Stormbringer*, I mean, Glenn can't help it. He likes the music that he likes and that was starting to change it. So it was starting to change from being a hard rock 'n' roll band to something that was becoming a little more funky, which Ritchie hated. And Ritchie, being true to himself just went 'that's it, I'm off. I don't like what's happening. I don't think I can get it back to what I wanted it to be' — and I think he saw the way that, 'If I have my own band, I can control it' and I think that's why Rainbow was formed."

Blackmore was quoted in *Sounds* in August 1975; "Once I'd done the album (*Ritchie Blackmore's Rainbow*) I realised that I was really excited about it. I found I'd enjoyed recording it a lot more than some Purple records. Well, let me qualify the statement, I enjoyed doing *In Rock* and *Machine Head* was pretty good as well. But I don't think there's been an album since then that I've really been excited about. So I thought that, to be honest with myself, I should really leave the band. We had another Deep Purple album coming up, you see, and I wasn't looking forward to it at all. I liked playing with Purple onstage because they were very good, but in the studio it took such a long time to get things together and it became a bit of a headache towards the end. So a few weeks before we were due to go into the studios I said no, I'd rather not. And that's when I split from the band. I just didn't like the way things were going. In the studio we'd be five egotistical maniacs, pushing the faders up so each of us would be progressively louder than any of the others. It wasn't a team effort anymore. The songs seemed to have been forgotten."

Blackmore was quoted of Rainbow in *New Musical Express* in August 1975; "There's more excitement, there's more enthusiasm because we're all new — I like Ronnie's voice very much, I like the way he can interpret what I play on the guitar — he seems to be able to integrate his melodies into my guitar progressions. We do use a lot of medieval modes, in the way that the modes work slightly differently to the scales. You use a lot of notes, whole tones... one prime example being 'Greensleeves' which was written in the sixteenth century by Henry VIII — or so he told me — or rather it was probably written by one of his court minstrels who he beheaded and stole the publishing rights from..."

Prior to its release, Blackmore was quoted of Rainbow's debut album in *Sounds* in April 1975; "I was thinking this is actually the most rewarding LP I've ever made. *Deep Purple In Rock* and *Machine Head* were good, this is another step forward for me after *Machine Head*. I'm playing very well and I think the songs are very good. I think it's great all round, I just hope people get to hear it. On this LP, it wasn't a case of 'I want to do my own LP' — that never came into it. People used to say 'well when are you going to do your own LP?' and I'd say 'well I'm doing it most of the time with Deep Purple anyway' well, I write most of the music, but I never had the time to do my own album."

There was a lot to be said for the strong musical rapport between Blackmore and Dio in terms of how Dio interpreted what Blackmore wanted to communicate on guitar. That's not to say that Blackmore and Coverdale didn't have a good musical connection, it's just that what Blackmore had with Dio probably had more strength to it due to their shared musical interests at the time. Blackmore was quoted in *Modern Guitars* in 1975; "I was really enjoying it because of his (Dio's) voice. When I played the songs to him, the way he interpreted them was he sings exactly where I would like to sing, if I could sing. The feeling is mutual as a guitar player. And he's got a really incredible way of getting a song across. I think his lyrics are brilliant. I think his timing is fantastic, his intonation, everything. And it's so hard to find a very good singer that can do that. It was always a hardship for me, not so much with Dave (Coverdale) and Glenn (Hughes), but there was always a barrier between the guitar and the vocal. I could never get across really what I wanted. They'd always interpret it their own way. And I thought, 'yeah, that's good.' We'd put it down and I'd go, 'yeah, it's okay.' But it was never, 'ah, that was great!' Whereas some of the songs on the (Rainbow) LP, most of them, have turned out exactly how I wanted them. He has an uncanny knack of knowing exactly what I want for some reason. I don't know how. So at the moment, I'm really pleased with what's going down."

Upon being asked why he didn't ask Ian Paice to come with him to be in Rainbow, Blackmore was quoted in *Modern Guitars* in 1975; "I had to get away from Ian for a time because Ian was partly going in a different direction. Ian is not into my medieval influences, pretty songs, sometimes songs with no rhythm to them. There must be rhythm as far as Ian's concerned. And he is the best drummer as far as rhythm goes. But, when you don't want rhythm, he's not prepared to put the song first. If there's no proper rhythm there, then there's nothing for him to do so he's not interested, not looking at it like, 'well, this is a valid song whether I'm playing or not.' That is why Ian is not with me."

Blackmore had put forward the suggestions of doing the Yardbird's 'Still I'm Sad' and 'Black Sheep Of The Family' by Quatermass on *Stormbringer*. It may have been the case that creatively, the songs weren't to the musical taste of the rest of Mk3 but also, there may have been some motive in play relating to the fact that doing other people's songs wouldn't have garnered royalties from a writing perspective. Whatever the reason was, it was certainly indicative of the fact that on *Stormbringer*, Deep Purple weren't working cohesively.

Both songs got the Ritchie Blackmore treatment on Rainbow's debut album. Blackmore was quoted in *Sounds* in February 1975; "I picked 'Black Sheep Of The Family' because it's a song I always wanted to do; it was done about three years ago by another band called Quatermass who are now friends of mine. Our group wouldn't do it because they said it wasn't original... it's just a favourite thing I wanted to do because there are some songs I just want to play even if they're not written by us. Sometimes too much shit comes out because everybody wants to write their own material. They say it's got to be original shit instead of copied good stuff. I think there are too many bands doing their own stuff and it's bad, they can't write. It's not like the old days when bands would do other people's stuff. Now everybody's doing their own material and it's getting very very boring. Too many groups are kind of getting away with murder."

In a strange kind of way Deep Purple's rejection of 'Black Sheep Of The Family' proved to be a strong catalyst for motivating Blackmore to go off and do some solo work; it was, after all, the first track that was recorded by the band that was due to be called (at least initially) Ritchie Blackmore's Rainbow. When asked, "I hear you're coming out with a solo single?" in Warner Bros.' November 1974 *Circular*, Blackmore was quoted; "I'm still working on it with a friend of mine who sings in a group called Elf and Matthew Fisher on organ. It's just a song I wanted Purple to do but the group refused to play it so I got together with some pals to do it. It's called 'Black Sheep Of The Family'. Nobody's ever heard of it. It came out on an album by Quatermass about four years ago. Everybody seems to be doing things on their own, so I thought I'd have a go."

Deep Purple's rejection of 'Black Sheep Of The Family', combined with the rapport between Blackmore and Dio, were vital ingredients for the beginning of Rainbow. Blackmore was quoted in *Modern Guitars* in 1975; "It started first of all with Roger Glover, or Clover, that's what we used to call him. He was a bass player with us in Deep Purple. He and Ian Paice had recorded and produced Elf and they told me they (the group) could use help. So it started with that. I had never heard the LP, but Roger and Ian both kept saying, you know, how good the band were. Then they were signed to Purple Records and it (Elf) came out soon after. Then we met them on the tour in America about three and half years ago, and they used to support us a lot on the American tours and we got to be friendly. I noticed in particular the singer. It was his style and the way he was singing. The rest of the band was very good, too. We got to be friends. But it wasn't really brought home to me how good a singer he (Dio) was until Barry St John. I don't know if you know Barry St John — she sings a lot on Pink Floyd and does sessions for all the big groups — said what a great voice he's got. And then I thought, 'yeah' because I hadn't really taken one hundred per cent interest. I had been like casually listening. I started listening and I said, 'yeah, that's really good.' I heard the song 'Black Sheep Of The Family', which is the single from the new Rainbow album, and I asked Purple if they wanted to do it on the next LP and they said they didn't want to do anybody else's songs. I really wanted to do this song. I had wanted to do it for the last two years. So, I said to Ronnie — I got him around one night and I got him drunk — 'do you fancy doing it?' and he said, 'yeah, I might sing it.' He got the song off in about a half an hour. Then we went into the studio and we put it down. It sounded great except for some of the musicians involved who weren't really musicians. That was what started it. Once I heard that, I thought, 'well, we're gonna need a B-side.' I just wanted to put it out as a single. No big deal. I just wanted to be involved in the song 'cause I loved the song so much. And we put a B-side down, which we wrote in a hotel when we were on tour. The song turned out so well, we didn't know which to put on the other side. So I thought, 'well.' We were all thinking the same thing at the same time — 'when are we going to make an LP then?' So we said, 'okay'."

On balance, Jon Lord remembered events differently. He considered it to be the case that when Blackmore played something in the sessions for *Stormbringer*, there were times when Deep Purple liked it but Blackmore said that they couldn't use it because he was saving it for his solo album. According to Lord, a similar thing had been happening since the making of Mk2's *Who Do We Think We Are*. Lord was quoted of Ritchie Blackmore in *Circus* in December 1975; "He's a difficult bugger, but that's part of his charm."

Still though, for Blackmore and Dio, leaving Deep Purple and Elf respectively was about opening a door of new creative opportunity. Dio was quoted in *Sounds* in April 1975; "I've really enjoyed taking part in this album. It's given me and the rest of the band a chance to do things we never really knew we were capable of before. This originally began when Ritchie wanted to cut a single, a version of 'Black Sheep Of The Family', a song he's wanted to lay down for a long while. We then wrote a B-side, 'Sixteenth Century Greensleeves', which turned out to be better than the A-side, so Ritchie decided to do an album, but he said he'd only do it if I did it with him. I couldn't believe it, it was like God asking me if I wanted to come to heaven. So here we are. Apart from rating Ritchie as a guitarist, I rate him as a person."

Blackmore was quoted of 'Black Sheep Of The Family' in the same feature; "I picked it because I've always liked the song since Quatermass first did it in 1970. A friend of mine used to play drums with them, Mick Underwood. Some people say 'yeah, I know why you chose that song.' I don't play a song because of its title. It was the thing that motivated the whole LP. Ronnie and I got together to do it, and I said let's do it because I knew he could do it well. Purple didn't want to do it, they like their own songs and this was written by someone else. We got into the studios and things worked out so well that I thought 'right, we've got to do a B-side now' — the B-side turned out better than the A-side and then I was tempted to do an album because I knew they wouldn't plug a single if there wasn't an LP to back it up."

David Coverdale was quoted in *New Musical Express* in August 1975; "Now he (Blackmore) can do exactly what he wants, I think he'll be happier now — he's got much more control with the people he's working with. Instead of turning round to Jon and telling him what to play and Jon saying 'I prefer it this way' he's got players who'll do exactly what he tells them to. They're good players too."

Starting Rainbow was probably more about Blackmore wanting to have control of the musical direction of the band he was in rather than wanting to elevate his status in terms of star persona. He was quoted of the Mk3 line-up in Warner Bros.' November 1974 *Circular*; "They're good. It's still five ego crazy musicians fighting for the spotlight, but that will always be there. If there were any problems it would be in that respect. Everybody wants to be the star. Well, I don't want to be the star as much as I want my music played and played right. I'm very domineering and pushy. I really couldn't care less about being the star, just as long as the star is doing my material. If I listen to someone else play music, if it doesn't grab me right off, I'll ignore it. I mean I could be a big guitar star and all but, in a way, that's best left to people like Jimmy Page, who look good in white suits. I always get embarrassed when I start flaunting myself. I could be very sexy on stage and all that business, but

## The End Of An Era?

it doesn't really turn me on. I think I'm being rather silly. If I start wiggling my hips, I do that for maybe half a minute and then stop. It's degrading."

When asked if he thought he would ever outgrow Deep Purple, Blackmore was quoted in the same feature; "Of course. The only question is how soon. It does get frustrating. You can practice till you're blue in the face and people will still miss the point. But as soon as I play the guitar with my feet they go, 'yeah, that's good' so you wonder whether it's worth it. Everyone seems to like this new album though. I don't know why but they all do. Glenn played it for David Bowie the other night. Bowie loved it. I don't know if that's a good sign or what." (David Bowie was in the studio with Glenn Hughes when he was recording the vocals for 'Hold On').

David Coverdale was quoted in *New Musical Express* in November 1974; "I get on very well with Ritchie, I accept him for what he is and he accepts me for what I am. And it's very successful when it comes down to writing. We have the same influences. I've also done some writing with Jon (Lord) this time, and we came up with some good ideas, the majority of which are not on the album. In fact, there's two. There's a song called 'Holy Man', and a thing called 'Hold On', which Mr Bowie I believe is interested in recording... He came round to see us a few times in LA and was very nice, and I think he said he was interested in doing that particular song. I'd be interested to hear what he does with it, 'cause it seems a little unusual for his taste."

Blackmore was interviewed in August 1975 by *New Musical Express* about him having left Deep Purple. When the interviewer stated that he had left the band three months prior to the interview, Blackmore was quoted, "Physically that is. Spiritually, I left about a year ago. I made the best of it. I was a bit tired of the ideas and the personnel — it was all a bit routine. But everybody's approaching their material in the same way. Most of the big bands I know are, most of them are very lazy. The way we used to approach making records was we would allot two weeks for rehearsals, then for maybe twelve days play football, and the other day we'd sleep, then we'd probably rehearse for one hour of the day that was left. We wrote most of the material in the studio, so it was a case of falling back on professionalism rather than creative... um... songs. I lost the excitement of it."

In the same feature, Blackmore was quoted on how he had a renewed enthusiasm about working with a different group of people in the form of his new band, Rainbow; "I've gained it (excitement) through being with different personnel. People used to say to me, 'When are you making a solo?' and I used to say, 'Well, I do that all the time with Deep Purple!' It was a case of I wanted to use different people... I found that quite honestly I was doing most of the work with Deep Purple myself — without sounding conceited — I just found that a lot was relying on me. So I thought, sod this..."

Blackmore was quoted in *New Musical Express* in August 1975; "Since *Deep Purple In Rock* it was written always by Roger (Glover), Ian (Gillan) and myself. Jon (Lord) would be very good at advising whether to use an A Major or a C Minor but he didn't write. That's another big reason why I left. There were no writers in the band — including myself. I can write to a degree but I do need help. Ian was always there — Ian Paice the drummer — he always had lots of adrenalin, wanted to get on with it and play — but a drummer can't contribute any more than playing the drums unless he's a songwriter and a piano player."

For context, all albums made with the Mk2 line-up of Deep Purple (*In Rock*, *Fireball*, *Machine Head* and *Who Do We Think We Are*) were managed in such a way that every band member had writing credits on every song of each album. This was done for diplomatic reasons. Blackmore was quoted in April

## The End Of An Era?

2015 in *The Guardian*; "I did most of the riffs and progressions because, basically, we had so many arguments in the first two years of Purple, and I was sick of it, so I said let's split it five ways, because everyone was bickering about 'I wrote that one note' (and) 'Include this song, which is a bunch of rubbish, but I wrote it' — every band goes through that. There's one thing today we haven't got over with modern technology. We haven't found a way to fashion a computer to take the information and tell you who's written the song. That would be very nice. People said to me, 'You were silly to split it five ways for most of it' but I said, 'Purple wouldn't have been together at all if I hadn't done that' because they were very strong-minded people. It would have died out in 1970 if I hadn't done that."

For the Mk3 line-up of Deep Purple, writing credits on songs were based on which individuals contributed to the process on each song. It comes across that this change in the method of writing was ultimately not to Blackmore's preference. That's not to say that things always ticked along nicely and happily in the Mk2 line-up (they didn't!) but the fact remains that post (and indeed during *Stormbringer*), Blackmore wasn't happy with how things were being ran in Deep Purple, both from a writing perspective, a musical one and perhaps, generally (as a number of his early Rainbow era interviews seem to suggest).

By the end of Deep Purple Mk3, it comes across that although everyone had remained professional and kept putting in a good performance from a musicianship perspective, from a personnel perspective, Blackmore had simply had enough. He wasn't engaged with Deep Purple creatively or socially by that point. He was quoted of the personal dynamics in the Mk3 Deep Purple line-up in *New Musical Express* in August 1975; "There were people who said we hated each other but I never let it get that far. Otherwise we'd have broken up a long time ago. I used to have my own dressing room because I like solitude before going onstage — I have four or five guitars to tune up and I can't do that with someone playing bass or organ in the same room. I prefer to be on my own. I'm a loner — not because I don't like people, it's just that I like to be alone because... uh... for instance... I find myself more interesting than most people I meet... It sounds pretty conceited... probably is... I dunno."

When asked if he was writing songs prior to joining Deep Purple, David Coverdale was quoted in *Record World* in June 1976; "I was writing a lot more consistently, funnily enough. It is really weird with Purple because when I got in and got over the initial nerve thing they were saying we've got you two new guys (myself and Glenn) and we want to change the style a little. We felt the same on listening to some of the older stuff, that it was getting very clinical and they wanted to try a bit more so I was bringing in a few ideas. When I was first playing them I got the impression from them of 'it doesn't sound like Purple' so consequently to please them and everybody else I started writing with Purple in mind, which was limiting to a certain extent because I like to write in various styles. At the moment, I'm in the process of writing songs for consideration by other artists. I'm getting back into consistency. I became dependant on Ritchie because I'd come up with good guitar licks but he would take them and expand them into something mind blowing — he's a genius — and my limited 'You Don't Know Like I Know' guitar riffs turned into phenomenal guitar excursions."

The creative freedom that Blackmore was probably aiming for was certainly recognised by *Billboard* when Rainbow's debut album was reviewed in August 1975; "Former Deep Purple lead guitarist and founder Blackmore joins with several members of Elf and this new group here is the result. As might be expected, Blackmore's guitar work is the highlight. He seems, however, to have mellowed a bit since his Purple days. The runs and riffs are a bit less rapid fire and a bit more tasteful. Vocalist Ronnie James Dio is a versatile singer who handles rockers and ballads equally well, thus allowing Blackmore the freedom to serve up some more subdued licks — a luxury he did not have often in Deep Purple. While the band is hard rock, the total effect is not quite as blasting as might be expected from the fusion of the Elf congregation and Blackmore. Several possible singles here."

Blackmore was quoted of Rainbow's first album in *Modern Guitars* in 1975; "Some of the songs could have been done by Deep Purple, but there's this sort of Bach influence in there, too. Maybe some Hendrix influence in there. But it's funny, it would have been a natural progression for Deep Purple in my opinion, but it wasn't. We went off on a tangent with funk, which didn't agree with me. It's not my thing, not my bag, man."

Blackmore was quoted of Mk3 Deep Purple in *Modern Guitars* in 1975; "It was great, then it just went to pieces again... I don't have any feeling toward Purple. I wish them the best of luck and I like them as people. We all still get along very well. They are all very intelligent, very nice people."

# Chapter Six

## Stormbringer Is A Worthwhile Album

Stormbringer* was reviewed in *Rolling Stone* in January 1975; "With *Burn* and now *Stormbringer*, Deep Purple has attempted to prove, firstly, that replacing the departed Ian Gillan and Roger Glover with David Coverdale and Glenn Hughes has in no way weakened the highly successful and profitable D.P. sound and, secondly, that to continue to sell albums the band need no longer rely on the unique but overdone speedo-riff rock that made the five albums from *In Rock* to *Made In Japan* quadrillion sellers. While the two newcomers are just as competent as their predecessors (as witnessed on the title cut, one of the few real throwbacks to *Machine Head* days), the attempts that the band has made at diversifying its sound have been only partly successful. While the group's 'Hold On' should rightly be considered one of the neatest, most accessible and rockiest songs they've ever done, slower paced stuff like 'Holy Man' or the Uriah Heep-like 'The Gypsy' hardly rate above the commonplace. *Stormbringer* still exhibits a few points of flash — the occasional familiar Blackmore riff or Lord organ wail — but in total it's a far cry from the band's peak."

Despite that in the charts, *Stormbringer* didn't fare as well as some of Deep Purple's previous albums, that's not to say that in the grand scheme of things, the album didn't do well. It only took a few weeks to go Gold in America (it was certified as such on 9th January 1975) and it stayed in the top twenty for twenty weeks. *Record Word* reported in February 1975; "Deep Purple's current Warner Bros. album, *Stormbringer*, has been certified Gold by the RIAA in recognition of sales in excess of one million dollars."

*Record World* reviewed *Stormbringer* in November 1974; "Certain to come in for a royal chart reign, this latest set from the British hard rockers rouses the senses with tasty musical flavours and enticing harmonies. Impassioned vocals are set upon equally fervid and cohesive riffs, with FM and top forty airplay as well as sales being a natural spin-off."

Glenn Hughes was quoted in Popoff's book, *Sail Away*; "When David and I came in, the band started to become more, and I'm going to say, soulful. Because we grew up in the North of England, we grew up listening to American R&B. Rather than try replacing Gillan and Glover with two look and sound-alikes, they replaced them with two totally different commodities, and it showed very strongly on *Stormbringer* what it was all about. And I like change in music. I don't want to make *Burn* II. Led Zeppelin did a really good job in their careers of making different records every time. So that's how I feel about *Stormbringer* — it's a different record."

On *Burn*, the solo sections on the album's title track are very much classically influenced passages in terms of the chord structure and rhythmic patterns. In such regard, the track is reminiscent of 'Highway Star'. The hard rock sound is still very much there, as is evidenced on 'What's Goin' On Here'. However, there are certainly some funk and soul type rhythms present on 'Lay Down, Stay Down' and 'Sail Away'. Essentially, I would suggest that *Burn* is still distinctively close to what Mk2 Deep Purple sounded like in terms of organ and guitar solos but equally, the soul and funk influences on some tracks are undeniable.

This puts *Burn* up there as an album that is demonstrative of the fact that whilst Deep Purple had an established sound that they maintained on many parts of the album, the funk and soul influences that ultimately became distinctive features on *Stormbringer* were already there in *Burn* but with Hughes more at the creative helm on *Stormbringer*, that would certainly explain the increase in funk and soul on that album.

*Stormbringer* was reviewed in *New Musical Express* in November 1974; "When you weigh it up, Deep Purple are in the most unenviable of positions — they have a certain reputation to live up to, right? Presumably in an attempt to retain the magical quality which obviously makes them more than another rock and roll band, they've maintained certain style characteristics that unfortunately never allowed them to develop musically. And even though they got themselves a new singer and bass player, their last album, *Burn,* was pretty much a predictable member of the Purple cycle, and certainly nothing innovatory. To an extent, *Stormbringer* follows a similar tactical plan. The title track is a roaring riff of clichés, which later reappear with variations of the barren 'Love Don't Mean A Thing' and the electronic groan called 'Lady Double Dealer'. And the rest of the album is, well, a damn sight better, with sparks of ingenuity occasionally lighting up like a hundred Ronson electronics clicked in unison. But the overall impression of the album is one of change — Deep Purple are slipping out of that worn and shiny cloak which is so easily recognisable. The most distinctive facet of their new image comes with such numbers as 'Hold On', 'You Can't Do It Right', 'Highball Shooter' and to a lesser degree, 'The Gypsy'. All these exude a laid back funkiness, no doubt an influence of black soul music. Perhaps the key phrase to this set is actually laid back. Glenn Hughes on bass and drummer Ian Paice rock steady throughout, laying down a meaty (though strangely non eventful) rhythmic tempo. 'Holy Man' is decidedly dull, and Paice and Hughes only become inventive on the last track of side one, 'Hold On'. In the same way, the vocal chords of

Hughes and David Coverdale complement the musical feel, except for some over-dramatisation from Coverdale which mars the finest composition of the set, 'Soldier Of Fortune'. It is probably Ritchie Blackmore who commands the majority of honours for this album. He is superb, placing neat, cohesive figures into 'Hold On', chopping fine rhythmic patterns on 'You Can't Do It Right' and easing through some deliberately mellow and refined lines on 'Love Don't Mean A Thing'. And Jon Lord is so laid back he doesn't make any significant keyboard contributions until the third cut on side two. More so than most of their previous albums, *Stormbringer* is quite a satisfying musical excursion, despite the criticisms I've already noted, and plus the fact that the lyrics are generally very ordinary. One should not, however, overlook the fact this is quite an adventurous album for Purple insomuch as it attempts to stay clear of tried and tested formulas. And the result, even if flawed, does at least partly enhance their musical credibility."

*Stormbringer* was reviewed in *Record Mirror* in November 1974; "Musically, *Stormbringer* is no great break through. The same familiar guitar riffs filter through the speakers as tight and concise as they ever were, proving that Deep Purple still are one of the leading lights in the schmashing (sic) heavy music. David Coverdale's vocals, though not as deadly a weapon as Ian Gillan's, are more soulful and maybe a little easier on the eardrums at four in the morning. He sounds particularly superb on tracks like 'The Gypsy' and 'Stormbringer', although it was a wise decision to give Glenn Hughes lead vocals on the serene (for Purple anyway) 'Holy Man', on which he sounds not unlike albino Johnny Winter's baby brother Edgar. The nimble-fingered Jon Lord still sounds dandy, really groping dem (sic) keys on 'High Ball Shooter'. Purple-ites should find this enjoyable, though I personally would have preferred something a little less predictable."

The fact that *Burn* was a difficult album to follow is

perhaps corroborated in how the album's title track was most often used as the opening number in Mk3's live sets. *Burn* had helped Deep Purple to weather the storm in early 1974 as the band quickly adjusted to a new level of success with David Coverdale and Glenn Hughes completing the Mk3 line-up. By the time of *Stormbringer*, Coverdale and Hughes were no longer the new people and as a result, they had more creative control over the band. Compared to *Burn*, *Stormbringer* is reflective of a very different working dynamic within the third line-up of Deep Purple. David Coverdale was quoted in *Disc* in November 1974; "Of course a lot of things have changed because of my involvement with Purple. I have become about one hundred and one per cent more confident for a start — my confidence has been amplified. I think I've matured musically, and I'm far more into what the band, as a whole, are doing. I'm very happy with the way things are progressing."

'Lady Double Dealer' and 'The Gypsy' don't seem too stylistically different to what Mk2 might have done. One is a hard rocker and the other is driven by sentimental lead guitar. It was reported in *Circus Raves* in January 1975; "Often Deep Purple's LP songs seem to fall together out of nowhere. Sometimes Jon Lord will write something on his own, or maybe Ritchie and Dave will get something together on guitar and piano at Ritchie's house. But Ritchie Blackmore's favourite track on the album, 'The Gypsy', was put together right in the studio as they were recording. It's got the most guitar of any song on the album, and features some playing which could be likened to that on 'Layla', quite the departure from the norm... It's about a fortune telling nomad who can see into the future, a lyrical departure from a band known for writing songs about nasty ladies and burning casinos."

Blackmore was quoted in the same feature; "I came out with a riff and then I followed it up, put in a chord progression, and let Dave have a go with the words."

Not all of *Stormbringer* is heavy on the funk and soul influences, but the tracks that are, are certainly in the majority. Overall, *Stormbringer* does contain a healthy amount of hard rock. The title track and 'Lady Double Dealer' present as such and there are also the more soulful pieces present too; 'Love Don't Mean A Thing', 'Holy Man', 'Hold On' and 'You Can't Do It Right (With The One You Love)'. And then of course, the album is closed nicely with the soft ballad, 'Soldier Of Fortune'.

There are instances in which it perhaps feels like Lord, Paice and Blackmore are all less musically engaged with *Stormbringer* purely on the basis that it is a less solo oriented album (Lord's solos on 'High Ball Shooter' not withstanding!) but to be fair, it comes across that less soloing was part of the initial remit when Deep Purple were deciding what to do for their post *Burn* album. Deep Purple weren't trying to do with *Stormbringer* what they had tried to do with, for example, *In Rock* in 1970 or *Machine Head* in 1972. Whilst the latter two albums were very much intended to be upbeat, rough and attention grabbing hard rock, *Stormbringer* was designed to be something different and that's okay.

In some ways, feeling frustrated that *Stormbringer* was so different to Deep Purple's earlier albums is futile because in the grand scheme of things, the album was reflective of a completely different stage in the band's tenure in terms of personnel and the musical interests present as part of that. Some may say that *Stormbringer* was disappointing due to the fact that it wasn't pioneering in the way that *In Rock* was but this is where it is probably worth asking, "does every album need to be pioneering to be of significance in a band's longstanding discography?" and "does it need to be pioneering in order to be enjoyable?" Overall, all members of Mk3 Deep Purple had a strong interest in creating interesting melodies (even Ian Paice as the drummer, when you consider how he complemented

Glenn Hughes' bass playing in the rhythm section).

It may have been the case that whilst making *Stormbringer*, melodic content was perhaps considered before the style it was to be played in. When asked if he had always wanted to be a rock singer in particular, David Coverdale was quoted in *Record World* in June 1976; "A singer, yes. I wasn't really bothered — I love many different kinds of music. Singing rock is a great physical and emotional release but it's very limiting to a certain extent because it's a constant screaming thing, particularly when you're in competition with some of the loudest players there are. At times it's frustrating because I can handle excellent melodies, but as I say, rock and roll doesn't call for melody. I'm very pleased to see Queen making it. Someone gave me a couple of albums the other day and I was playing some of them to my lady and she said their sense of melody is immaculate. It's very confusing, there's very little you can latch on to, there's a phrase here and there you can pick up, but it's very clever rock and roll."

Coverdale was quoted in *New Musical Express* in November 1974; "I'll be honest, and I don't want NME cynicism, but I never considered being a rock and roll star and I never wanted to be, and I don't consider it now although it gets drummed into me occasionally. I wanted to be a purveyor of good music. Like, my record collection is excellent, displaying many tastes, all of which have got something to do with — not soul, but feel. I have things by John Williams, Sergio Mendes, Miles Davis and Otis Redding — anything I can interpret; anything I can identify with."

Essentially, when writing a song, if an artist prioritises getting a good melody together, the musical genre in which the melody is presented may come as something of a secondary interest and both Coverdale and Hughes had strong interests in funk and soul music from the very early days of their musicianship; writing in such a genre was a very natural choice for them both. It was noted in *Melody Maker* in February 1975; "Hughes' absorption of black music is especially evident in his bass lines of *Stormbringer*, Purple's latest album, and if the new record is any indication, the fivesome should continue the upward trend musically that *Burn* marked. *Burn* was a good album, Ian Paice noted, and *Stormbringer* is *Burn* grown up."

Coverdale was quoted in *Sounds* in November 1974 as he advocated of his influences and musical process from the age of fourteen; "I was singing through a Dynatron tape recorder complete with more feedback than we have now. Those were really heady days, it was terrific. There was no depth, if you know what I mean, nothing to be explored. We were all very limited. I don't think my voice had broken. And that's when I first learnt how to sing with my stomach, which sounds silly, but it's totally different from a normal voice. I remember we did 'Gimme Some Lovin'' and 'That In D'. I started singing it high without really thinking. That was before my throat had been bastardised with cigarettes and whiskey. The band just stopped and said 'you sound like Stevie Winwood' — which was just the stomach thing, using your mouth like a box, it was just amazing. From then on, I started working on that voice and one day I was listening to Alan Freeman's *Pick Of The Pops*, which was a Sunday religion and he played a version of 'Yesterday' by Ray Charles which had me in tears. I was on my own and I just went apeshit. I'd heard the Beatles version but this had the hairs standing on my neck. I thought it must be good to have a voice like that and that sort of feel. I started thinking 'I'm a person, I can feel and I can be hurt but why can't I emphasize it in what I'm doing' — that's when I started borrowing records and started listening to more than the Pretty Things, if you know what I mean. Going beyond the R&B thing." (A quick note about where Coverdale described singing from his stomach… It basically provides a vocalist with the scope to get a lot more depth and power behind their voice because they can use more of their body to get the sound and indeed feeling out of. Certainly, singing from the diaphragm, rather than just using a head voice, would give a vocalist much more opportunity to diversify their sound both technically and emotionally in terms of colour and tone — perfect for some of the more soul influenced tracks on *Stormbringer*).

Whilst the change of musical direction on *Stormbringer* is largely attributed to Hughes and Coverdale, not long after the album's release, there is evidence that Coverdale was open to doing a more rock oriented album as Deep Purple's next one. Having read Blackmore's opinions of *Stormbringer* in an earlier issue, Coverdale was quoted in *Sounds* in March 1975; "The next album's gonna be an out and out rocker. I agree with Ritchie. *Stormbringer* was too much of a transition. People want to hear Purple the way they've always been and that's what they're gonna get. I think I'll have a bash at a single."

Perhaps Coverdale was expressing an interest in doing a single to go in a musical direction that was different to that which was expected from Deep Purple. However, all that said, the funk and soul influences are certainly evident on *Come Taste The Band* but it fairness, that's not to say that the album is without its hard rock moments. Either way, the well ploughed narrative surrounding *Stormbringer* typically represents Coverdale as being one of the main advocates for making the album funky but on balance, he was a versatile musician who was open to exploring a range of musical styles, just as everyone else in Deep Purple was.

Glenn Hughes was quoted of his soul music influences in *Sounds* in January 1974; "I think it was the way I was brought up really, because I missed out on all the Shadows, the rock and roll and was brought up with Tamla (Motown) and soul and that's how I was brought up to play."

He was quoted in *Sounds* in November 1975; "I started playing guitar when I was fourteen and I did this for four years until someone asked me to play bass on a gig. From then on I got more into bass playing, although I kept up with the guitar and still play it with Purple. I just learnt by getting into it and listening to Stax people like Booker T and Marvin Gaye. I used to listen to Hendrix and Clapton as well but I was always more influenced by soul."

David Coverdale was quoted in *New Musical Express* in November 1974; "I adapt from everybody who I like and it's stored in my memory banks, and I use licks from everybody who's made an impression on me, which goes from Rod Stewart to Robert Johnson, Bobby Blue Bland, B.B. King, Albert King and so many other black cats. There are not really many white people I appreciate."

Upon the interviewer stating that *Stormbringer* was a "Motown-sounding album" Blackmore was quoted in *Sounds* in February 1975; "Yeah, unfortunately, I don't like that. We just did it; I like black people who can sing rock and roll but I don't like black music funk. It bores me to tears. But this is as far as it goes now, it's the end of that. Back to rock and roll next LP."

Furthermore, the funk and soul influences were familiar territory for Glenn Hughes; he had been playing such style of music previously with Trapeze. It was reported in *Sounds* in January 1974; "For people who aren't too familiar with Trapeze, they were a three-piece comprising of Mel Galley (guitar), Dave Holland (drums) and of course Mr Hughes (bass/vocals). The band originated as a five piece and released an album on Threshold. The strongest feature on the first effort was the powerful harmonies. The group eventually diminished to a trio and their second album — *Medusa* — was a start to the funky rock-soul feel they had. Trapeze proved to be fairly successful in parts of America, especially Texas where they shared their fans with ZZ Top, another hot three piece who were very close friends of theirs. They even had a chart entry in the

States, 'Black Cloud', from the *Medusa* album, but alas they were cruelly ignored in Britain. Even when the media buzzed with excitement on the release of their last and best album *You Are The Music, We're Just The Band*, there was still no flicker of hope for this ill-fated outfit."

Upon being asked who his musical influences were, Glenn Hughes was quoted in *Record World* in June 1976; "I have to say overall, Stevie Wonder was, and still is, but I've played with a lot of interesting people since. I met Stevie Wonder about three years ago but before that, I was really a big fan of his. I went into the studio with him and watched him. I also jammed with him and it was great, but before that everything that Stevie has ever done has rubbed off on me a lot, which is noticeable I suppose in some of the Trapeze material I used to do. It doesn't show so much with Purple because I haven't got that sort of commitment to do that, but I hope to do a solo album which David Bowie might produce. We've been talking about it for two years. David was staying with me in LA for two months, planning this album. So my personal songs will be coming out on that. As I say, Stevie Wonder overall is my major influence, but lots and lots of black artists are really what it is for me."

Hughes was quoted of Stevie Wonder in *Sounds* in March 1975; "He was really knocked out with the *Stormbringer* album. He came up to me and said, 'hey man, you bin stealin' mah licks' referring to 'You Can't Do It Right (With The One You Love)'. He really liked it!" Hughes stated of the song in his autobiography; "Love this song. This is the song I played Stevie Wonder when I met him at the Record Plant."

Hughes was quoted in *Sounds* in November 1975; "Feeling is the first thing you need when you're learning and even if you've got feeling, you also need the will to do it. When I left school I just knew I was going to be a pro musician — a twenty four hour musician, which is what I am now. Mind you, I never wanted to be a star particularly, and I still keep well clear of the business side of things. That can be a bit of a problem, last year I got ripped off by someone to the tune of $100,000. It's not a bad idea to have some feeling for the business as well as music, for this reason... As well as singing, I'm playing guitar and bass onstage, and guitar, bass and piano in the studio. I like to think of myself as a musician rather than a bass player. I enjoy all three so much, and now I think I've got a feeling on all three. Bass playing in particular is a feeling."

Whilst each member of Mk3 may have felt restrained that they didn't have as much musical control as they may have wanted on *Stormbringer*, the range of musical interests present in the group by that point probably went in the album's favour; the end product offers plenty of varied points of interest, all of which were played by talented musicians at the top of their game. As a fan, perhaps ignorance is bliss as in, the tensions within the band when they made *Stormbringer* certainly don't compromise what can be enjoyed when listening to the album. It would perhaps be all too easy to dismiss *Stormbringer* as not being a very worthwhile album; It's the album that led towards Ritchie Blackmore leaving the band, and that can't be a good thing can it? Well, actually, let the album speak for itself. Realistically, there is no way of measuring the extent to which personal frustrations put a downer on *Stormbringer* for him as an artist and in such regard, that weight isn't something that needs to be carried by fans when giving *Stormbringer* a listen.

Blackmore was quoted in *Modern Guitars* in 1975; "I'm an extremist. I like really hard rock, medieval music, or out-and-out ballads. I don't like this in between cool, laid-back, so-called music that people like. What most of the Americans are putting out these days I don't like. I can't stand it. It's also music to talk over. It doesn't grab you at all. I just get real irritable in most clubs and walk out. I like music that demands your attention and this (*Ritchie Blackmore's Rainbow*) certainly does demand you to either say, 'Great' or, 'It's terrible.' It's the same way as Deep Purple's *In Rock* and *Machine Head* (made you feel). And *Burn* to an extent. 'Mistreated' was good on *Burn*."

*Stormbringer* prompts an interesting question in terms of, "how can Deep Purple's music be defined?" Blackmore was quoted in *Sounds* in August 1975; "Purple seemed to be getting funky, especially with *Stormbringer*. I just don't like that sort of music. It was all becoming too classy, too laid back and cool. That's not Deep Purple. Deep Purple are a brash, demanding band. Don't get me wrong, I don't just like hard rock. I like hard rock, classical and ultra melodic things. But I just don't like funk music. I hear it all day and night in America and I'm sick of it all."

So that was Blackmore's definition of what Deep Purple's music should be and understandably, many fans probably subscribe to that too. In such case, it is understandable as to why a lot of fans might not think too well of *Stormbringer* but again, a lot probably comes down to expectations in the case of that album. That said, surely no band would want to come to a standstill in terms of creative progression. When asked if he considered it a mistake to have replaced Gillan and Glover with Coverdale and Hughes, Blackmore was quoted in the same feature; "Not necessarily. I didn't say that. I don't think Purple could have gone on doing that type of music (Mk2) forever. It (Mk3) was a good break. But now, with Rainbow, I want to carry on the music and expand upon the essence of Deep Purple — aggressiveness, but with a kind of medieval feel to it. It's hard to explain. My album isn't that much different to what Purple were doing at the time of say, *Machine Head*. Perhaps it's indicative of the direction I would have liked Purple to go on after that album, if I'd had more control."

It was advocated of *Stormbringer* in *Circus Raves* in January 1975; "The new Deep Purple album is a thundering work, full of excitement and energy that's buoyed the group through its many crises, yet there's a new element present in the group's sound. There's a lyrical maturity and a sense that they're searching for something beyond their past achievements. This, after all, is what great bands are all about."

Lyrically, *Stormbringer* is an interesting album because it deals with such a broad spectrum of ideas and subjects. Whilst it is not my place to make a feeble attempt to interpret them, there are a lot of points of interest. With the title track, there's the sense of the mythical and yet, other tracks on the album deal with more sentimental (but relatable) day to day subjects such as 'You Can't Do It Right (With The One You Love)', 'Love Don't Mean A Thing' and even, to a point, 'Soldier Of Fortune'. Lyrically, *Stormbringer* showcases themes of the surreal and adventurous as well as the romantic and philosophical. That's quite an achievement for an album that was made under an extent of personal tensions within the band.

It is worth noting that whilst there is often a strong case made that only Blackmore wanted to embrace fantasy themes in lyrics (as is evidenced on most of the songs on Rainbow's first album), it was Coverdale who contributed the idea of a "Stormbringer". He was quoted in Martin Popoff's 2015 book, *Sail Away*; "Oh my God! I wrote two songs which could be termed heavy metal or whatever. I've never embraced the term "heavy metal" because all my themes are emotional. But I wrote two songs to keep Ritchie Blackmore happy which were 'Burn' (which I still think is a classic) and 'Stormbringer' which basically if you look at the lyrics, they are more or less sci-fi poems. But it never felt comfortable for me to have those. In fact, I think that's where he got the name Rainbow from, the hook in 'Stormbringer'. 'Burn', I can enjoy any time of the day but I don't really go for 'Stormbringer'." (Of course, it is now known that Blackmore and Dio named their band after a bar that they liked to drink in).

Decades after *Stormbringer* was made, Jon Lord said in a

filmed interview; "The title track, it's a great rock song, you know, it's another terrific Blackmore riff. But again, lyrically, not my cup of tea. What is a Stormbringer actually? I'm not terribly sure. I'm being a bit sniffy about it but it's not my cup of tea lyrically, but it's a terrific track."

Blackmore was quoted of the subtleties in Deep Purple's music in Warner Bros.' November 1974 *Circular*; "If people are clever enough, they'll catch them. If they don't, that's too bad, it's their tough luck. We're not geniuses. Nobody, well, there's been a few around. Hendrix was a genius for about three years, then he went downhill. Cream put out some great stuff for about two years. McCartney's doing it. Paul Rodgers is a genius. But so often, people just miss the point. As soon as they hear anything loud, they go, 'well this is heavy metal rubbish' yet when they hear a folk band playing, they go, 'well that's nice' — it's all very stupid."

David Coverdale was quoted in *New Musical Express* in November 1974; "I wrote the lyrics about a mythical creature called Stormbringer who, in a surrealistic story, creates a lot of trouble. It's similar to the idea of 'Burn' but I never even considered Michael Moorcock's work. In my mind, I'd created the character called Stormbringer, which also could have come from my childhood interest in mythology. Thor, the God of Thunder had a hammer called Stormbringer, didn't he? (he didn't!). But mythology was another fantasy for me. I always imagined myself at the Pass of Thermopylae — you know, being a hero like the three hundred Spartans who defended Greece or something. Before I became a rock and roll star I could answer all the Greek mythology questions on *University Challenge*. Not bad for a fourteen year old, eh? It was a fantasy I could indulge in. I was fortunate because I lived in a large house, which was part of a working men's club, and I had what I called my music room. It was an enormous room in which I used to build all sorts of constructions like Roman galleys. I'd indulge in a terrific fantasy with friends of mine who shared all this."

*New Musical Express* advocated in the same feature; "It was only when he (Coverdale) showed the lyric to another member of the band that a comparison to the Moorcock work ("Stormbringer" is the name of a fearsome sword) was made. Then when David arrived home from Munich, where the album was recorded, he discovered some of Moorcock's novels among a trunk of paperbacks." Coverdale was quoted in the same feature; "People indulge in fantasies, I'm quite sure you do. I've got them. I go and see *Dirty Harry* or *Magnum Force* and I think Clint Eastwood's hot, and come out feeling a little drab. Or I see Bruce Lee and think 'Oooh, I wouldn't mind having a go at that' — A fantasy is something you create in your mind. I'm very against violence, but I would love to have the power to sort out half a dozen guys if they started pissing about with somebody. You need that fantasy because day-to-day life is dreary. What upsets me is people think there's so much bloody glamour in this business. But it's about time people realised there isn't so much glamour. The fantasy of that glamour thing, like the old Hollywood, is necessary to a lot of people. I don't mean the supposed glamour that's supposed to surround us when we have press receptions or anything like that. The glamour is when you walk on stage and you have thousands of kids going crazy. Audience reaction is the best dope in the world. It's the greatest high I've ever had in my life. But I didn't experience it until Copenhagen last year when I did my first gig with Purple."

Prior to joining Deep Purple, Coverdale had done entry level sales jobs and been on social security. It is highly likely that when making *Stormbringer*, he was giving it his all. He was quoted in *New Musical Express* in November 1974; "I've been given an opportunity which I've grasped firmly with both hands, which anyone would do, for a certain amount of financial security for a certain amount of years, I'd be a fool not to. I'm now able to indulge in choices — to eat fish and chips or to eat sirloin steak. Or to go to London for a couple of days and stay in a hotel — rather than sleep on a bench. Which I've done, by the way. I'm into the material thing because my biggest bloody pain years ago was financial insecurity. How the hell could I fall in love and say to the chick, 'Come and live with me at my mother's and she and my father will take care of you because I'm a die-hard musician'? The only way I think I've changed is I've got a lot more confidence — One hundred and one per cent instead of ninety nine. I rely so much on human relationships — male and female. Male for communication and female for physical."

Coverdale was quoted of his relatively newfound fame with Deep Purple in *Disc* in November 1974; "Naturally there are some disadvantages. I often find that the people I like are put off by finding out what I do now, while the sort of people I don't like are attracted to me because of it."

In the same feature, Coverdale was quoted on what it was like going back to his hometown as a famous person; "I try to get up there as often as I can, but that's not very often I'm afraid. And when I am there I have the problem that people think you're different even if you aren't."

When it came to making *Stormbringer*, Coverdale was very much an appreciated member of Deep Purple when it came to the fans. He was quoted in *Disc* November 1974; "There are some real bums in this business — but there are also some very nice people, I'm so lucky because all the people in the band are great. All our roadies are really nice guys too. When there are so many people touring round together, as there are with this band, you're so lucky to find a crowd who get on well. Going on the road is such a performance — it's like uprooting four Dagenhams every time you move from one gig to another! I think the worst thing is that you have no real contact with the audience when you play such enormous gigs as we do. Half the time people at the back can't even see you. And you very seldom get a chance to meet any of the audience. I'll never forget one night when we did. Some blind people were brought backstage to meet us. That had a profound effect on me. There was this one girl who touched my face all over just so that she could really feel what I looked like. When she was talking to me, she explained how much she enjoyed Purple's music and how much she got from 'Mistreated' (on *Burn*). That was a track that I wrote and she really got through to me. I'll never forget that — or her." Whilst Coverdale and Hughes weren't part of the nucleus of Deep Purple's founding musicians, they had earned their place as part of the band's legacy.

It could be argued that Coverdale's and Hughes' influence on *Stormbringer* was problematic in how they took the reins that little bit more than Blackmore would have liked. Surely Deep Purple were meant to be hard rock and (as much as it divides opinion) heavy metal? Realistically though, Coverdale and Hughes have always been strong musicians in their own right; with them having significantly contributed to the success of *Burn*, it would have probably been unfeasible to expect them to humbly continue seeing themselves as the new guys.

In the interests of being fair, it might not be the case that Coverdale and Hughes were being domineering during the making of *Stormbringer*; the fact is that Blackmore had explored the possibilities of a solo career long before the Mk3 line-up of Deep Purple. It may have been the case that nobody was being excessively domineering and that Blackmore had sat back a bit due to having lost interest by that point. There would have inevitably been a risk in leaving Deep Purple to start a new band, particularly when Deep Purple were commercially doing so well, but Blackmore had already abandoned starting a new project in 1971 when he and Ian Paice did a studio session with Phil Lynott under the band name of Babyface. The recording never saw the light of day. Essentially, one of the main reasons that the project was abandoned was owing to the fact that it was felt that it was too much of a risk to leave Deep Purple and start again with a new band. Ritchie Blackmore was quoted in *Sounds* in February 1974; "I wanted to get my own band together, with Phil Lynott and Ian Paice because we've always stuck together. We thought we'll get this together and start again more or less. I asked Jon what he was doing. He was going to go with Tony Ashton and I said I'm off to make a rock band like Deep Purple and Paice is coming with me. Ian (Paice) said it would be silly to abandon our years' efforts. I thought it would be an adventure, but finally agreed that it would be silly starting from scratch."

By 1975 though, Blackmore had a strong reputation as an individual and although it would have still been a risk to leave Deep Purple, he was in a better position to take a gamble. As was reported in *Circus Raves* in January 1975; "The dark brooding fretmaster's way of disposing of guitars had been a subject of bitter controversy among the rock-going public. He never did just smash them, but threw them up in the air a few times, gave 'em the old "Blackmore Dance Lesson", played them with his feet, scraped them across the heads of the front row onlookers, fret them with bottles of wine while splashing the liquid over them and then dashing them on the amplifiers. But the sensationalistic string-sado also just happened to be acclaimed as one of the finest guitar players this side of Jeff Beck, admired and imitated by more than a few pickers."

Blackmore was quoted in *Sounds* in August 1975; "To tell you the truth, I've been thinking about leaving the band for a couple of years, whether I had a band of my own or not. I think a lot of the members of Purple thought that because I had an album in the can I was leaving. It wasn't like that at all. I left because I was tired of doing certain things, I'd lost enthusiasm and I was fed up. So I'd been thinking of leaving for a long time. I was just being lazy and kept putting it off and picking up the dollars — another day, another dollar, as they say. But when this came along, I just knew it was the right time. I might return to being a pauper, but at least it's honest and something I'll always be is honest. I think maybe…"

It seems that there was a lot of mutual respect and admiration for each other's musicianship in the early days of Mk3 Deep Purple. Glenn Hughes was quoted in *Sounds* in January 1974; "I've always rated Ritchie for years, Ian Paice completely knocked me out when I saw him. Jon I've always admired as a musician, too, but when I saw him play I couldn't hear him so I couldn't feel what he was playing. But now I can hear him the stuff he plays is absolutely knockout especially on the album. I can't describe working alongside him because he's so precise he never makes a mistake. Ritchie's the greatest improviser I've seen since Hendrix. He gets a bit pissed off because he knows he's good but doesn't go round telling everybody in print. It's a bit sad when people go round saying Beck and Ronson are the best and nobody mentions Blackmore."

It is vital to recognise that as much as the disagreements on *Stormbringer* were about genre and style, the mutual respect that Mk3 Deep Purple had for each other as musicians didn't seem to diminish. Glenn Hughes stated of 'The Gypsy' in his autobiography; "I like Blackmore's haunting vibes on the guitar, and there's a real Lennon/McCartney vibe to the song. It's a fans' favourite."

When asked if he considered his playing on *Stormbringer* to be more lively than on previous Deep Purple albums, Ritchie Blackmore was quoted in Warner Bros.' November 1974 *Circular*; "I don't think so. I don't think there's as much life in it this time as before. You'll always get this though. Some people say it's good, some people say it's crap. I always go by an average of songs that turn out decently. It's hopeless for me to try to turn on in the studio."

When it came to making *Stormbringer*, the frustrations within Deep Purple were probably more about the writing than the playing of the music. Musically, everyone was established to an extent that was largely unquestionable but it was in the writing that Mk3 just couldn't seem to agree. Glenn Hughes stated of 'Stormbringer' in his autobiography; "One of the few songs that Blackmore came up with for the album was this one. It's a very straightforward, Deep Purple sounding song. David says 'Your mother sucks cocks in hell' on it, the line from *The Exorcist*. We'd been to a private showing of the movie."

There has often been a strong case made for the idea that *Stormbringer* was radically different from anything that Deep Purple had done before. But was it really? David Coverdale was quoted of *Stormbringer* in *Disc* November 1974; "There are a lot of changes but it's still the Purple everyone knows."

*Cash Box* reviewed *Stormbringer* in November 1974; "Heavy makes you happy, cried the Staple Singers and suddenly there was Deep Purple filling the need for millions (over fifteen million worldwide) of heavy metal fans who needed the sound to stay happy. The Deep Purple story is one of much dues paying and the ultimate reward in the form of superstardom. *Stormbringer* is an LP in true Purple tradition, rich with riffs, boisterous with vocals that ride a subcurrent of bass lines like a surfer on a thirty footer and material directed at the young at heart. A certain top ten LP, we look for 'Lady Double Dealer' and 'Love Don't Mean A Thing' to hit big."

Really, the review is largely agreeable in terms of how *Stormbringer* is "rich with riffs" and it is "boisterous with vocals". And well, whether it is heavy metal or not is debateable simply because the definition of heavy metal itself is tremendously debateable. Also, Deep Purple have long been appreciated for their music on the basis of what it offered melodically and certainly, *Stormbringer* isn't really an exception in such regard. It was reviewed in *Disc* in November 1974; "I cannot tell a lie.

I have always been a great fan of Deep Purple, which makes me more than a little biased when it comes to reviewing their albums. Nevertheless, I think this is one of the best they've made since *Machine Head*. There are some extremely strong numbers on it, which after a couple of hearings feel like old friends. 'Holy Man' is one and 'The Gypsy' is another, but there's so much good material that it's difficult to single out one or two superlative tracks. Purple's music has changed since the replacement of Gillan and Glover with Coverdale and Hughes. In a feeble attempt to define the change all I can say is that the music is now slightly less dramatic and more melodic, but just as memorable as ever. Now that the new line-up has stabilised they are producing some fine music — if this is the shape of things to come, roll on the next album."

*Stormbringer*'s title track is in line with the heavy rock that Deep Purple were known for. As the opening track, if the whole album's following songs were in the same style, then *Stormbringer* would have been an album that sounded more like what people were expecting from Deep Purple.

*Cash Box* reviewed the 'Stormbringer' single in February 1975; "Featuring the thunderous sound of Deep Purple, this song is a real flurry of rock and roll. Lightning fast guitar against pounding bass and drums swirl around the ominous vocal. Blowing hard like a gale, this song is bound to overwhelm you."

I could be entirely wrong, but I'm not convinced that the person who reviewed the single actually listened to it. Whilst description of music is always going to be subjective, 'Stormbringer' has a pretty steady pace, the guitar isn't particularly "lightning fast" and it's more of a steady hard rock than rock and roll. Equally the drum part doesn't have that much bass in it. To me, the review reads like someone took a good stab of a guess at what the song might sound like based on the title of it and what they were already aware of in terms of Deep Purple's work or at least, their musical reputation. Still though, if my theory is right, it would certainly be in line with the case that by 1975, Deep Purple were of such significance that *Stormbringer* was in a good position for selling well purely on the reputation of their previous work. Maybe the reviewer did listen to the track and was keen to put lots of storm related words in their description.

Blackmore was quoted in *Disc* in August 1975; "I thought for a long time that Purple were not being honest with their fans — as you must know, it's not so much how you play as how they think you play. They seemed to be trading on their reputation and I don't like that. Whatever happens I want to be honest with the people who buy the records even if it means that I have to start again right (or almost) from the beginning."

In November 1974, *Radio & Records* noted simply of *Stormbringer*, "Tremendous following. Guaranteed to be a hit." The review isn't very clear as in, does it mean that Deep Purple have a tremendous following and therefore an album by them will do well. Or is the review getting at the idea that *Stormbringer* in and of itself already had a strong following. Either is plausible due to the speed at which the album reached Gold status in America. I advocate that the former probably holds weight on the basis of the California Jam having taken place just seven months earlier.

Although Blackmore has often said that the soul and funk aspects of *Stormbringer* weren't to his preference, there was perhaps also a sense that he didn't necessarily want to strongly advocate for making music that was strictly in the vein of hard rock by that time in his career. It may have been that the concept of Deep Purple had become a bit of a monster; media and fan expectations had perhaps made the band feel restricted in what they were able to create — obliged to adhere to what many had come to consider to be Deep Purple's sound as a result of the supposed remit set out in their previous albums.

Blackmore was quoted in *New Musical Express* in August 1975; "We did have a channel we had to keep to — or producing hard rock all the time. I love hard rock. It was my idea to do it, along with Ian (Gillan) and Roger (Glover), but we couldn't stray from it very much or people would go 'It's not as hard as their last one' or if we did do a hard rock thing the press would always go 'Huh, same old thing. Heavy Metal Rubbish' which they never saw the subtleties of. And of which they never will do. They'd rather talk about folk singers. But that's another thing... The subtleties were what was involved in the simple structure of the song, incorporating such a limiting structure. To have to make up good solos in that structure is very hard. People would hear a riff and say 'Oh, that's kids' stuff' but it's not as simple as that. And you can make music in seven-four or five-four but it's easier than making four-four if it's not different, the content. For instance, the solos count on a lot of the songs. That was the subtlety of most of the songs."

It comes across that Blackmore had had enough of the musical style that was expected of him in Deep Purple. He was quoted in *New Musical Express* in August 1975; "All the music I play at home is either German baroque music — people like Buxtehude, Telemann, or it's medieval music. English medieval music. I prefer things like the harpsichord, the recorder and the tambourine... Whenever I'm pissed off with the rock scene, which is quite often, I just tune in to Bach, play my Bach records and medieval music and people come round — like other artists — and it's so funny, the reaction that you get. They think 'Ah, rock musician, Gold records on the wall' expecting all the funk shit to come booming out — shoeshine music — and on comes medieval tambourine dancers and jigs... and Bach."

Coverdale was quoted of *Stormbringer* in *Sounds* in November 1974; "There's three tracks on the new album that are definite Purple, because they have a definite sound because there's always been the nucleus of Ian, Jon and Ritchie. We don't write songs to suit a Purple audience, we write songs that we like and it happens that the audience get off on them. There's no contrivance there. You can't change the Deep Purple, you can put a different vocal on top of it and you can use different approaches to material."

With a distinctive riff and powerful playing from everyone, *Stormbringer*'s title track sets the tone of the album in terms of the talent in the band. Straight into the second track, 'Love Don't Mean A Thing', it becomes apparent that *Stormbringer* is a move away from playing with aggressive power, particularly when, as a point of comparison, looking back to the opening track of *In Rock*, 'Speed King'. The same applies with *Stormbringer*'s third track, 'Holy Man'; there is a sense of tenderness and sentimentality to the song. But this doesn't mean that *Stormbringer* isn't an enjoyable album in terms of, "does everything have to be hard and heavy to be considered as good rock?" and "what's wrong with a sense of strong emotion in rock music?". Besides, Deep Purple were never without that in their music in the days of Mk2, for example, 'Child In Time' on *In Rock*.

'Hold On' is a groovy number so the beginning of side two, 'Lady Double Dealer', is once again a change in style. The eclectic choice of music genres on *Stormbringer* comes across very strongly when you consider that both side one and side two of the LP start with tracks that are hard rockers before taking such an explicit change of direction. 'Lady Double Dealer' is a powerful Deep Purple track because it features a distinctive riff and strong, fast and powerful virtuoso playing throughout (as is particularly the case in Jon Lord's organ playing on this track). The absence of extended solo passages in 'Lady Double Dealer' is not to its detriment as a song that is melodically very memorable.

'You Can't Do It Right (With The One You Love)' has Deep Purple's move towards funk written all over it. But again, it is melodically memorable and again, includes a distinctive riff. In such case, yes it is demonstrative of a change in Deep Purple's sound by that point in their tenure but in terms of the fact that the song is reflective of five musicians playing very well and with energy, it's a worthwhile song. *Cash Box* reviewed the single, 'You Can't Do It Right (With The One You Love)' in November 1974; "Culled from their newly released *Stormbringer* LP, the masters of heavy rock come across with a moderate paced rocker that will infect you with a great hook. Some excellent riffs are complemented with some fine vocals and background harmonies. Strong disc from Purple who have positively done it right. Watch and see!"

'High Ball Shooter' is also reflective of a band who play well together with ease. It is followed by the beautifully executed piece, 'The Gypsy'. Side two concludes in a softer vein with the ballad, 'Soldier Of Fortune'. It was considered in *Circus Raves* in January 1975; "One song that Ritchie and David Coverdale wrote for the new album, 'Soldier Of Fortune', seems to be an indication of the new roads that Deep Purple has been taking. Rather than a stormy path, this tune moves along smoothly, guided by sailing Mellotrons and guitars showing nary a sign of turbulence. Hit by a bolt of what could well be religious inspiration, Deep Purple produced a hymn of our time, loaded with melody and a sound unlike the band has produced in years."

The general mellowness of side two (after the first two tracks) could easily invite the criticism of "it's not classic Deep Purple! It's not hard rock because it's not loud, brash and aggressive all the way through!" but really, does it have to be? With the talent that all five individuals brought to the Mk3 line-up, wouldn't it be rather peculiar if they made an album that tried to mimic some of the classic Mk2 albums such as *In Rock* and *Machine Head*?

I'm not convinced that it would have been realistic to expect

*Stormbringer* to fit into any sort of specific mould. Post *Burn*, Mk3 had proven themselves as being commercially viable to a tremendous extent and in such case, that could have easily presented them with the scope for maximum creativity. With the fan base established, the door was open to perhaps feel comfortable to experiment a bit and with the talent in that band, why, artistically, would anybody want to stand still? But stand still they didn't, and that's ultimately why Blackmore moved so far as to leave Deep Purple and start Rainbow.

# Stormbringer - A Comprehensive Discography

## *Album Personnel*

**Deep Purple**
David Coverdale - lead vocals (all but 'Holy Man'), backing vocals
Ritchie Blackmore - lead guitars
Jon Lord - organ, keyboards, electric piano
Glenn Hughes - bass guitar, lead vocals (all but 'Soldier Of Fortune'), backing vocals
Ian Paice - drums, percussion

*Credits*
Produced by Deep Purple and Martin Birch
Recorded at Musicland Studios, Munich in August 1974
Engineered by Martin Birch, assisted by Reinhold Mack and Hans Menzel
Additional recording and mixing by Martin Birch and Ian Paice, assisted by Gary Webb and Garry Ladinsky at The Record Plant, Los Angeles during September 1974
Mastered at Kendun Recorders, Burbank, California

# Track Listing

## *Side One*

Stormbringer (Blackmore, Coverdale) 4:03

Love Don't Mean A Thing (Blackmore, Coverdale, Hughes, Lord, Paice) 4:23

Holy Man (Coverdale, Hughes, Lord) 4:28

Hold On (Coverdale, Hughes, Lord, Paice) 5:05

## *Side Two*

Lady Double Dealer (Blackmore, Coverdale) 3:19

You Can't Do It Right (With the One You Love) (Blackmore, Coverdale, Hughes) 3:24

High Ball Shooter (Blackmore, Coverdale, Hughes, Lord, Paice) 4:26

The Gypsy (Blackmore, Coverdale, Hughes, Lord, Paice) 4:05

Soldier Of Fortune (Blackmore, Coverdale) 3:14

# Country By Country

This list includes all releases for the UK, USA, Japan and Germany as well as unusual versions released in other territories.

## UK
*Original November 1974 releases:*
Purple TPS 3508, LP
Purple TC-TPS 3508, cassette *
Purple 8X-TPS 3508, 8 track cartridge **

*The running order is different to the vinyl, as follows:

Side One
Stormbringer
Hold On
Holy Man
High Ball Shooter

Side Two
Lady Double Dealer
You Can't Do It Right (With the One You Love)
Love Don't Mean A Thing
The Gypsy
Soldier Of Fortune

**The running order is different to the vinyl, as follows:

Programme One
Stormbringer
Hold On

Programme Two
Holy Man
High Ball Shooter

Programme Three
Lady Double Dealer
You Can't Do It Right (With the One You Love)
Love Don't Mean A Thing (Part 1)

Programme Four
Love Don't Mean A Thing (Conclusion)
The Gypsy
Soldier Of Fortune

*Original CD release:*
EMI CDP 7 91084 2, 1989

*Reissues:*
Purple Records / Universal 3635858, LP 180 Gram, 29th January 2016
Purple Records / Universal TPS 3508, LP purple vinyl, 7th September 2018

*Remastered expanded releases:*

### EMI TPSX 3508, CD/DVD, February 2009
35th anniversary release. The CD contains the original album remastered with bonus tracks: Holy Man / You Can't Do It Right / Love Don't Mean A Thing / Hold On / High Ball Shooter (Instrumental)
*With the exception of High Ball Shooter, all the bonus tracks are remixes done by Glenn Hughes.
The DVD contains the quadraphonic mix of the album as originally released in the USA only.

### EMI TPSD 3508, 2LP, February 2009
Vinyl version of the 35th anniversary release including all the tracks as per the CD.

## USA

*Original November 1974 releases:*
Warner Bros PR 2832, LP
Warner Bros DEP M5P 2832, cassette
Warner Bros DEP M8P 2832, 8 track cartridge*
Warner Bros WST 2832-C, open reel

*The running order is different to the vinyl and is as follows:
Programme One
Stormbringer
Hold On

Programme Two
Lady Double Dealer
You Can't Do It Right (With The One You Love)
The Gypsy (Beginning)

Programme Three
The Gypsy (Conclusion)
Love Don't Mean A Thing
Soldier Of Fortune

Programme Four
Holy Man
High Ball Shooter

*Quadraphonic releases:*
Warner Bros PR4 2832, LP, 1975
Warner Bros DEP L9P 2832, 8 track cartridge, 1974
Warner Bros WSTQ 2832-QF, open reel, 1974
The quadraphonic mix not only produces a different sound, but it includes a different vocal take of 'Soldier Of Fortune'.

*Original CD release:*
Metal Blade Records 9 26456-2, 1990

*Remastered releases:*
Friday Music 829421-10562-6, CD, 2007
Friday Music FRM-2832, LP limited edition repress, 2012
Warner Bros R2 554989, 2CD, 2016

## Japan

*Original release:*
Warner Bros P-8524W, LP, 1974
The first 50,000 copies came with a poster. The OBI reflected that. Later copies had a different OBI.

Warner Bros YSA1031W, cassette, 1974

*Reissues:*
Warner Bros P-10110W, LP, 1976
With a red OBI similar to the original release.

Warner Bros P-6510W, LP, 1981
The OBI for this release is blue and orange.

Warner Bros 20P2-2609, CD, 10th February 1989
Warner Bros WPCR-873, CD, 10th October 1996
Warner Bros WPCR-1572, CD, 15th May 1998
Warner Bros WPCR-75039, CD, 22nd June 2005
Warner Bros WPCR-12267, CD, 22nd March 2006
Warner Bros WPCR-13116, CD, 17th September 2008
Warner Bros WPCR-78067, CD, 24th July 2013
Warner Bros WPCR-80221, CD, 24th June 2015
Warner Bros WPCR 17193/4, 2CD, 27th April 2016

## Germany

*Original release:*
Purple 1C 062-96 004, LP, 1974
Purple 1C 244-96 004, cassette, 1974

*Reissues:*
Purple 1C 072-96 004, LP, 1977
Purple 1C 038-79 1084 1, LP, unknown*
*The second reissue has a barcode making it post 1980.

## Other country releases on different labels:

### Greece
Harvest TPS 3508, LP, 1974
Although Purple Records was formed in late 1971 with releases throughout Europe from Machine Head onwards being released on Purple, for some reason Greece continued to release the albums on Harvest although they used the Purple Records catalogue number.

### Philippines
Parlophone TPS 3508, LP, 1974
Released on Parlophone but like Greece they also used the Purple Records catalogue number.

### Colombia
Odeon 11384, LP, 1974

### Turkey
Stateside TLS 23, LP, 1975

### Mexico
EMI SLEM-560, LP, 1975

### Uruguay
Odeon SURL 21555, LP, 1976
Title in Spanish on the cover — Traetormentas.

### Egypt
EMI 87-77056, LP, 1977

### South Korea
Oasis Record Co. OLE-444, LP, 1983
Unique release with the album called Soldier Of Fortune and the title track omitted, so side one only has three tracks. The Korean Ministry of Culture at the time had strict rules as to what was acceptable and clearly 'Stormbringer' wasn't deemed suitable for Korean consumption. Even more bizarre, the cassette version still used the cover with the word Stormbringer on it. To balance up the running times, side 1 of the cassette opens with 'Soldier Of Fortune (Reprise)'. Possibly the only time in history that a reprise has come before and not after!

# SINGLES

There were five different single couplings released around the world of tracks from the album, although no single was released in the UK.

**You Can't Do It Right (With The One You Love) / High Ball Shooter**
Warner Bros PRS 8049, November 1974, USA / Canada

**Lady Double Dealer / You Can't Do It Right (With The One You Love)**
Warner Bros P-1353W, 1974, Japan
Warner Bros P-143W, 1976, Japan
Warner Bros WPCR-1591, 1998, Japan (CD)

**Stormbringer / The Gypsy**
EMI 491, 1974, Guatemala

**Stormbringer / Love Don't Mean A Thing**
Warner Bros PRS 8069, January 1975, USA / Canada
Purple 1C 006-96 368, Germany 1975
Purple 2C 004-96368, France 1975
Purple 3C006-96368, Italy 1975
Purple 3C 000-70037, Italy 1975 (Jukebox release)
Purple 4 C 006-96 368, Belgium 1975
Purple 6C006-96369, Denmark 1975
Purple SPUR-88821, Yugoslavia 1975
Purple PUR 802, New Zealand 1975
Purple PURJ 90, South Africa 1975
Purple SMSOD-8953, Chile 1975
EMI 7705, Mexico, 1975
Odeon 01.01.472, Peru, 1975
Parlophone, PAL 64116, Philippines, 1975

*Although some of the 'Stormbringer' releases are often listed as 1974 because of the production date on the label, it is more than likely that they were all released in 1975, licensed as they would have been by Deep Purple (Overseas) Ltd.

## Soldier Of Fortune / Stormbringer
Purple Records – 4PUR 9004, Venezuela, 1975

# Mk3 Tour Dates

This is a full list of concerts performed during the period of MK3's existence. Concerts in grey were earmarked but cancelled.

## October 1973
Thursday 4th   Circus Kronebau, Munich, Germany
Friday 5th   Sporthalle, Cologne, Germany
Saturday 6th   Sportpalast Ahoy Rotterdam, Netherlands

These concerts were part of the *Rock Meets Classic* event where Jon Lord was invited to perform his *Gemini Suite* alongside with the Munich Chamber Orchestra, conducted by Eberhard Schöner. The rock musicians that Lord called upon were Glenn Hughes and David Coverdale, making these shows the first live performances together for Deep Purple's newest members although the second night was cancelled. The other musicians were Tony Ashton (keyboards), Pete York (drums), Purple recording artist Yvonne Elliman (vocals), Ray Fenwick (guitar) and Roxy Music's Andy MacKay (saxophone).

## December 1973
Saturday 8th   Stadion Hallen, Aarhus, Denmark
Sunday 9th   K.B. Hallen, Copenhagen, Denmark
Tuesday 11th   Gothenburg, Scandinavium, Sweden
Friday 14th   Forest-Vorst National Brussels, Belgium
Saturday 15th   Festhalle, Frankfurt am Main, Germany
Monday 17th   Olympiastadion, Innsbruck, Austria

With Aarhus cancelled, Copenhagen was the first MKIII show. For all six gigs the support act was Purple Records signings Tucky Buzzard.

## January 1974

| | |
|---|---|
| Sunday 20th | Palais des Sports, Paris, France |
| Tuesday 22nd | Fair Exhibition, Hall 16, Strasbourg, France |
| Wednesday 23rd | Palais des Sports de Besancon, Besancon, France |
| Friday 25th | Messehalle, Sindelfingen, Germany |
| Saturday 26th | Philipshalle Düsseldorf, Germany |

## February 1974

| | |
|---|---|
| Saturday 9th | Big Surf Arena, Tempe, Arizona, USA |
| Sunday 10th | Forum, Inglewood, California, USA |
| Monday 11th | Long Beach Arena, California, USA |
| Tuesday 12th | Sports Arena, San Diego, California, USA |
| Friday 15th | Tarant County Convention Centre, Fort Worth, Texas, USA |
| Saturday 16th | Civic Centre Coliseum, Amarillo, Texas, USA |
| Friday 22nd | Metropolitan Sports Centre, Bloomington, Minnesota, USA |
| Sunday 24th | International Amphitheatre, Chicago, Illinois, USA |
| | Big Surf Arena, Tempe, Arizona, USA |
| Monday 25th | International Amphitheatre, Chicago, Illinois, USA |
| Tuesday 26th | Freedom Hall, Louisville, Kentucky, USA |
| Wednesday 27th | Long Beach Arena, California, USA |

**All the February dates were announced but cancelled and in some cases rearranged.**

# March 1974

| | |
|---|---|
| Sunday 3rd | Cobo Hall, Detroit, Michigan, USA |
| Monday 4th | Cobo Hall, Detroit, Michigan, USA |
| Tuesday 5th | Memorial Auditorium, Buffalo, New York, USA |
| Wednesday 6th | Civic Arena, Pittsburgh, Pennsylvania, USA |
| Friday 8th | Capital Centre, Largo, Maryland, USA |
| Saturday 9th | Cumberland Memorial Arena, Fayetteville, North Carolina, USA |
| Sunday 10th | Coliseum, Charlotte, North Carolina, USA |
| Monday 11th | The Omni Stadium, Atlanta, Georgia, USA |
| Wednesday 13th | Madison Square Garden, New York, USA |
| Thursday 14th | Veterans Memorial Coliseum, New Haven, Connecticut, USA |
| Friday 15th | Spectrum, Philadelphia, Pennsylvania, USA |
| Sunday 17th | Nassau Coliseum, Long Island, Uniondale, New York, USA |
| Monday 18th | War Memorial Auditorium Syracuse, New York, USA |
| Tuesday 19th | Gardens, Boston, Massachusetts, USA |
| Wednesday 20th | Civic Centre, Providence, Rhode Island, USA |
| Friday 22nd | University of Daytona Arena, Dayton, Ohio, USA |
| Saturday 23rd | Dane County Memorial Coliseum, Madison, Wisconsin, USA |
| Sunday 24th | International Amphitheatre, Chicago, Illinois, USA |

| | |
|---|---|
| Monday 25th | International Amphitheatre, Chicago, Illinois, USA |
| Thursday 28th | Coliseum, El Paso, Texas, USA |
| Saturday 30th | Tarant County Convention Centre, Fort Worth, Texas, USA |
| Sunday 31st | Civic Centre Coliseum, Amarillo, Texas, USA |

**April 1974**

| | |
|---|---|
| Monday 1st | Tarant County Convention Centre, Fort Worth, Texas, USA |
| Tuesday 2nd | UNM Arena, Albuquerque, New Mexico, USA |
| Wednesday 3rd | Denver Coliseum, Denver, Colorado, USA |
| Thursday 4th | Denver Coliseum, Denver, Colorado, USA |
| Saturday 6th | California Jam Ontario, Motor Speedway, California, USA |
| Sunday 7th | Big Surf Arena, Tempe, Arizona, USA |
| Tuesday 9th | Sports Arena, San Diego, California, USA |
| Wednesday 10th | Tucson, Arizona, USA |
| Thursday 18th | Caird Hall, Dundee, Scotland |
| Friday 19th | Odeon Theatre, Edinburgh, Scotland |
| Sunday 21st | Apollo, Glasgow, Scotland |
| Monday 22nd | Apollo, Glasgow, Scotland |

# May 1974

| | |
|---|---|
| Friday 3rd | Odeon Theatre, Birmingham, England |
| Saturday 4th | Odeon Theatre, Birmingham, England |
| Sunday 5th | Guild Hall, Preston, England |
| Monday 6th | Trentham Gardens, Stoke-on-Trent, England |
| Thursday 9th | Hammersmith Odeon, London, England |
| Friday 10th | Theatre Royal, Norwich, England |
| Saturday 11th | Theatre Royal, Norwich, England |
| Sunday 12th | Lewisham Odeon Theatre, London, England |
| Tuesday 14th | Odeon Theatre, Newcastle, England |
| Wednesday 15th | King's Hall, Belle Vue, Manchester, England |
| Friday 17th | Kursaal Ballroom, Southend-on-Sea, England |
| Saturday 18th | Gaumont Theatre, Southampton, England |
| Sunday 19th | Winter Gardens, Bournemouth, England |
| Monday 20th | Colston Hall, Bristol, England |
| Wednesday 22nd | Kilburn State Gaumont, London, England |
| Thursday 23rd | Brangwyn Hall, Swansea, Wales |
| Friday 24th | Civic Hall, Wolverhampton, England |
| Saturday 25th | Kursaal Ballroom, Southend-on-Sea, England |
| Sunday 26th | Capitol Theatre, Cardiff, Wales |
| Tuesday 28th | Coventry Theatre, Coventry, England |
| Wednesday 29th | Coventry Theatre, Coventry, England |

## June 1974
Saturday 1st  Herkulessaal, Munich, Germany
Monday 3rd  Circus-Krone, München, Germany (two shows)

These concerts were part of the *Rock Meets Classic* event where Jon Lord performed his *Windows Suite* alongside with the Munich Chamber Orchestra, conducted by Eberhard Schöner. The other musicians were Glenn Hughes and David Coverdale, Tony Ashton (keyboards), Pete York (drums) and Ray Fenwick (guitar).

Thursday 27th  Kursaal Ballroom, Southend-on-Sea, England

## July 1974
Saturday 27th  Santamonica Rock Festival, Rimini, Italy

## August 1974
Saturday 24th  Orange Bowl Stadium, Miami, Florida, USA
Monday 26th  Dillon Stadium, Hartford, Connecticut, USA
Thursday 29th  Arrowhead Stadium, Kansas City, Missouri, USA
Friday 30th  Astrodome, Houston, Texas, USA

## September 1974

| | |
|---|---|
| Wednesday 18th | Stadthalle, Bremen, Germany |
| Friday 20th | Olympiahalle, Munich, Germany |
| Saturday 21st | Grugahalle, Essen, Germany |
| Sunday 22nd | Neue Messehalle Nuremberg, Germany |
| | Weser-Ems-Halle, Oldenburg, Germany |
| Tuesday 24th | Halle Münsterland, Münster, Germany |
| Wednesday 25th | Deutschlandhalle, Berlin, Germany |
| Friday 27th | Rhein-Neckar-Halle, Heidelberg, Germany |
| Saturday 28th | Festhalle, Bern, Switzerland |
| | Tauber-Frankenhalle, Würzburg, Germany |

## October 1974

| | |
|---|---|
| Thursday 17th | K.B. Hallen, Copenhagen, Denmark |

## November 1974

| | |
|---|---|
| Wednesday 13th | Cow Palace, San Francisco, California, USA |
| Friday 15th | Memorial Coliseum, Portland, Oregon, USA |
| Saturday 16th | Seattle Centre Coliseum, Seattle, Washington, USA |
| Sunday 17th | Pacific Coliseum, Vancouver, Canada |
| Wednesday 20th | Long Beach Arena, California, USA |
| Thursday 21st | Selland Arena, Fresno, California, USA |
| Friday 29th | Olympia Stadium, Detroit, Michigan, USA |

## December 1974

| | |
|---|---|
| Sunday 1st | Cincinnati Gardens, Cincinnati, Ohio, USA |
| Monday 2nd | Market Square Arena, Indianapolis, Indiana, USA |
| Tuesday 3rd | Kiel Auditorium Convention Hall, St. Louis, Missouri, USA |
| Thursday 5th | International Amphitheatre, Chicago, Illinois, USA |
| Friday 6th | The Coliseum, Cleveland, Ohio, USA |
| Monday 9th | Metropolitan Sports Centre, Bloomington, Minnesota, USA |
| Wednesday 11th | Arena MECCA, Milwaukee, Wisconsin, USA |
| Thursday 12th | Freedom Hall, Louisville, Kentucky, USA |
| Friday 13th | Greensboro, North Carolina, USA |
| Saturday 14th | Veterans Memorial Coliseum, Jacksonville, Florida, USA |
| Sunday 15th | Carolina Coliseum, Columbia, South Carolina, USA |
| Tuesday 17th | Scope Coliseum, Norfolk, Virginia, USA |
| Wednesday 18th | Civic Centre, Baltimore, Maryland, USA |

## January 1975
Saturday 25th — Sunbury Festival, Melbourne, Australia

## March 1975
Sunday 16th — Palata Sportova Pionir, Belgrade, Yugoslavia
Monday 17th — Sportska Dvorana, Zagreb, Yugoslavia
Thursday 20th — Brøndby Hallen, Copenhagen, Denmark
Friday 21st — Scandinavium, Gothenburg, Sweden
Sunday 23rd — Westfalenhalle, Dortmund, Germany
Tuesday 25th — Sporthalle, Böblingen, Germany
Thursday 27th — Friedrich-Ebert-Halle, Ludwigshafen, Germany
Saturday 29th — Sporthalle, Cologne, Germany
Sunday 30th — Ernst-Merck-Halle, Hamburg, Germany

## April 1975
Thursday 3rd — Bundeseisstadion Liebenau, Graz, Austria
Saturday 5th — Saarlandhalle, Saarbrücken, Germany
Monday 7th — Palais des Sports, Paris, France

# In-depth Series

The In-depth series was launched in March 2021 with four titles. Each book takes an in-depth look at an album; the history behind it; the story about its creation; the songs, as well as detailed discographies listing release variations around the world. The series will tackle albums that are considered to be classics amongst the fan bases, as well as some albums deemed to be "difficult" or controversial; shining new light on them, following reappraisal by the authors.

*The first four titles published were:*

| | |
|---|---|
| Jethro Tull - Thick As A Brick | *978-1-912782-57-4* |
| Tears For Fears - The Hurting | *978-1-912782-58-1* |
| Kate Bush - The Kick Inside | *978-1-912782-59-8* |
| Deep Purple - Stormbringer | *978-1-912782-60-4* |

*Other titles in the series:*

Deep Purple - Slaves And Masters
Emerson Lake & Palmer - Pictures At An Exhibition
Korn - Follow The Leader
Jethro Tull - Minstrel In The Gallery
Kate Bush - The Dreaming
Elvis Costello - This Year's Model
Deep Purple - Fireball
Talking Heads - Remain In Light
Jethro Tull - Heavy Horses
Rainbow Straight Between - The Eyes
The Stranglers - La Folie